T0291322

Structural Transformation and Sustainable Development in the Global South

This book investigates the relationship between sustainable development and structural transformation within international development policy. On the one hand, sustainable development is promoted as a multi-dimensional concept for achieving environmentally and socially responsible change. On the other hand, structural transformation refers to a sustained period of growth in living standards and incomes that brings sectoral change. For some, these two objectives seem at odds with each other, but this book argues that incorporating environmental initiatives into structural transformation goals in lower-income countries actually results in better results than strategies prioritising economic growth. Drawing on extensive structural equation modelling and original analysis, the book presents an innovative inclusive sustainable development framework to demonstrate the benefits of a more integrated approach to development planning, aiming for structural transformation in line with inclusive sustainable development principles.

This book will be of interest to students and researchers of global development, and to policymakers within government and development organisations.

Seung Jin Baek is a South Korean Economist of the United Nations, specialising in the political economy of sustainable development, where he primarily focuses on knowledge production for the provision of evidence-based advisory services to the Member States on development plans, strategies and frameworks. He holds a PhD from the University of Bath, UK.

Routledge Explorations in Development Studies

This Development Studies series features innovative and original research at the regional and global scale. It promotes interdisciplinary scholarly works drawing on a wide spectrum of subject areas, in particular politics, health, economics, rural and urban studies, sociology, environment, anthropology, and conflict studies.

Topics of particular interest are globalization; emerging powers; children and youth; cities; education; media and communication; technology development; and climate change.

In terms of theory and method, rather than basing itself on any orthodoxy, the series draws broadly on the tool kit of the social sciences in general, emphasizing comparison, the analysis of the structure and processes, and the application of qualitative and quantitative methods.

Women-Owned SMEs in Emerging Markets
The Missing Link in Global Supply Chains
Shabnam Shalizi

Rethinking Copyright for Sustainable Human Development
Higher Education and Access to Knowledge
Sileshi Bedasie Hirko

Structural Transformation and Sustainable Development in the Global South
An Integrated Approach
Seung Jin Baek

For more information about this series, please visit: www.routledge.com/ Routledge-Explorations-in-Development-Studies/book-series/REDS

Structural Transformation and Sustainable Development in the Global South

An Integrated Approach

Seung Jin Baek

Routledge
Taylor & Francis Group
LONDON AND NEW YORK

First published 2022
by Routledge
2 Park Square, Milton Park, Abingdon, Oxon OX14 4RN

and by Routledge
605 Third Avenue, New York, NY 10158

Routledge is an imprint of the Taylor & Francis Group, an informa business

British Library Cataloguing-in-Publication Data
A catalogue record for this book is available from the British Library

Library of Congress Cataloging-in-Publication Data
A catalog record has been requested for this book

ISBN: 978-1-032-19586-5 (hbk)
ISBN: 978-1-032-19588-9 (pbk)
ISBN: 978-1-003-25991-6 (ebk)

DOI: 10.4324/9781003259916

Typeset in Times New Roman
by Deanta Global Publishing Services, Chennai, India

Contents

Figures

Tables

Boxes

Preface

Over the past two years or so, humankind has had to struggle with an unprecedented historical shock, namely the COVID-19 crisis, and while this is not the first pandemic the world has had to face, it has been labelled by some as the "most challenging crisis since World War II." In this regard, today's pandemic will be regarded as a world-formative event because of its effects on humanity, both in terms of desire and ability, which will ultimately determine the social order, the way of life and even the system of world relations. Of course, it is also clear that this crisis will eventually come to an end and pass somehow. But what is even more clear is that our world before and after the pandemic will be markedly different.

Although the COVID-19-related socioeconomic damage appears to be concentrated on developed countries whose economic contraction is estimated at 4.6 per cent in the pandemic year of 2020 whereas the figure is minus 2.1 for developing countries, the reality might be quite different. In other words, much of the developing country group, or the so-called "Global South," whose national statistical systems often remain unsystematic, especially during the pandemic era, may have suffered far worse from the COVID-19 devastation than advanced nations.

By admitting, if you will, that this developing group may have just begun to reap the benefits of globalisation and neoliberalism over the past three or four decades and in fact has made remarkable economic progress, wouldn't it seem that the COVID-19 crisis is now "kicking away the ladder"? Besides, doesn't it seem that strengthening national medical systems and quarantine capacity to deal with the pandemic in a timely manner may all be just pie in the sky as their focus is clearly fixed on climbing up the economic ladder?

Notwithstanding such complex and uncertain dynamics affecting the Global South, all we need is to stick to the basic development principle, which is to take one step forwards at a time, realising the aspirations of sustainable development and structural transformation. This is indeed the chief reason why I am driving this humble work. In this context, the book investigates the interaction between sustainable development and structural transformation as development policy goals and outcomes, with particular reference to low-income countries. This entails simultaneously examining two overlapping policy agendas, both aimed at moving away from an exclusive focus on economic growth.

- The first is a global normative agenda to promote sustainable development as a multi-dimensional concept, combining indicators of economic growth, income inequality and environmental sustainability.
- The second is a context-dependent national agenda to achieve structural transformation, incorporating geographical and sectoral changes in resource allocation and use in order to reduce dependence on the current international division of labour.

An overarching framework for integrated analysis of these two development agendas, referred to as the Inclusive Sustainable Development (ISD) framework, is developed. The focus is then narrowed to empirically investigate trade-offs and synergies between the pursuit of economic growth, increased income equality, environmental sustainability and indicators of structural transformation by the use of structural equation models with a data set comprising 29 countries in Africa as a representing group for the Global South.

My investigation suggests that a compartmentalised approach – *grow first, redistribute and clean up later* – reduces the potential for long-run structural transformation. It further emerges that a strategy of incorporating environmental initiatives into Africa's structural transformation goals outperforms one that prioritises economic growth, while a strategy favouring social development goals may be most effective in the context of structural transformation.

Overall, the outcomes of the book suggest that the structural transformation of low-income countries can benefit from an integrated approach to development planning, set out as a model for the ISD framework. Realising this potential depends on sustained investment in national planning capability to integrate, prioritise and sequence policy interventions aimed at structural transformation in line with the three dimensions of inclusive sustainable development.

Having explored complexities surrounding development policies towards sustainable structural transformation, this book is primarily aimed at students and researchers of social sciences, including, but not limited to, economics, sociology, political science, jurisprudence international development, anthropology and history. The main findings of the book should also be accessible to readers with a general interest in the evolution of human society and people seeking inspiration, perhaps of a revolutionary mind, who seek guiding principles in a sometimes threatening new world.

As I am approaching the end of my writing, I would profoundly like to thank Dr James Copestake and Dr Aurelie Charles for their intellectual guidance and constructive criticisms. I am also indebted to Helena Hurd and Matthew Shobbrook, the excellent editorial team at the Routledge, and the anonymous reviewers for their invaluable comments that helped me substantially in the development of the book. Furthermore, the authorisation by the United Nations for the publication of this book is also gratefully acknowledged. It should however be noted that this book is published in my own capacity and not as a representative of the United Nations.

Finally, and most importantly, I would like to thank Youri Lee whose support, encouragement and unwavering love were undeniably the bedrock upon which the past decade of my life has been built. She is my wife, best friend and mother of my beloved children, Harynn Baek, Yoojoon Baek and Ryeorim Baek.

1 Policy dilemmas for structural transformation to be sustainable

1.1 Contemporary policy mix

Over the past half a century, the world has experienced rapid changes. Indeed, during this time, the world economy is estimated to have expanded nearly 4.5 times, which can be translated to mean continuous annual average growth of over 3 per cent worldwide.[1] But behind this trajectory, ideas about development have been in a state of constant flux, with influential thinkers driving a never-ending evaluation of development discourse – incorporating theories of modernisation, endogenous growth, globalisation and neoliberalism, among others.[2]

The upward trend in aggregate economic growth has also been associated with diverse experiences depending on the context and level of development (see Figure 1.1).[3] For instance, economies of developed countries have expanded over the same period at about three times larger in gross domestic product (GDP). In terms of per capita GDP, this group reached US$39,185 in 2020, which is nearly four times greater than the world average of US$10,891. Their contribution to global economic growth was about 57 per cent in 2020, although this had shrunk by 25 percentage points, from 82 per cent recorded in 1970.

Likewise, many developing countries have also made remarkable progress in sustaining positive growth over the last five decades, while also improving their performance in social indicators such as health and education. Real GDP volume in developing countries increased by 1,067 per cent between 1970 and 2020, which is about 2.5 times the global increase over the same period of 449 per cent. These economies are increasingly referred to as forming the new growth engine of the world as many of them are growing more rapidly than developed countries in the Global North.[4] Measured by GDP volume on average, the difference between the two groups decreased from 4.6 to 1.4 times over the period 1970–2020.[5] Hence, such *catching-up* or *economic convergence* across countries has

DOI: 10.4324/9781003259916-1

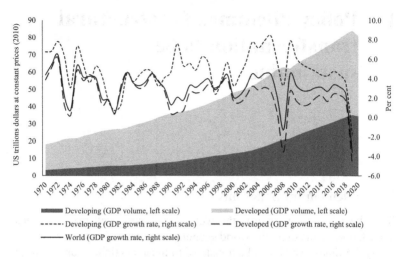

Figure 1.1 Historical improvement of economic growth: developed versus developing countries, 1970–2020. Source: Author's own elaboration on the basis of UNCTAD (2021). Note: The underperformance of the year 2020 can be considered exceptional, mainly due to the negative effect of the COVID-19 pandemic.

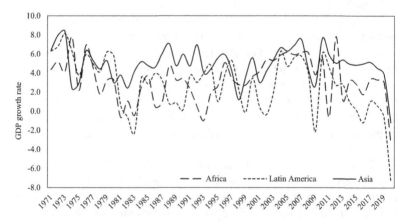

Figure 1.2 Heterogeneous growth performance of developing countries: Africa, Latin America and Asia, 1971–2020. Source: Author's own elaboration on the basis of UNCTAD (2021).

been observed in the trajectory of global development since the 1970s (Maddison, 2008).

It should however be noted that growth performance within developing countries has been very heterogeneous (see Figure 1.2) and will further be very different from each other mainly due to the COVID-19 crisis and its multi-dimensional repercussions to society (see Box 1.1[6]). Among developing countries, Asian countries have sustained the greatest economic growth record with a 4.9 per cent average over the period 1971–2020. This averaged growth rate is far greater than that of Africa and Latin America (3.3 per cent and 2.8 per cent, respectively). Asia's remarkable performance may have largely been attributed to the development trajectories of the four Asian Tigers (i.e. Hong Kong, Singapore, South Korea, and Taiwan), who realised a radical growth while attaining a manageable level of inequality (Sachs and Warner, 1997; Parente, 2001).

BOX 1.1 META-DISCOURSE ON THE COVID-19 CRISIS AND BEYOND

Over the past months and year, the entire world has suffered from a shutdown, self or institutional quarantine, the collapse of medical systems, teleworking challenges, economic downturn and many other developments to which we had previously given little thought, if any. Nonetheless, we have also proved ourselves in terms of having the resilience, determination and solidarity to overcome such hardships observed across many countries in the world. What we have confronted and gone through together has given rise to new perceptions and emerging trends in the fields of politics, economy, industry, education, health and the environment. In other words, it has become clearer that we, the people, should respond proactively rather than fear the upcoming "new normal." We need to unravel our new way of viewing the future we are facing; explore several potential policy considerations at the national level; and dissect the likely-to-be redefined future narrative of the post-COVID-19 era.

1.1.1 Smart government for a newly redefined national security context

Despite its many uncertainties, the COVID-19 crisis is arguably an ideal opportunity to redefine the role of the state (EBRD, 2020; Greer et al., 2020). We have clearly observed and sometimes experienced that the safety of people is directly affected by the governance and institutional quality of individual governments. In parallel, citizens will have more room to tolerate any form of state intervention if it helps to ensure their lives and safety. During its crisis response, national governments seem to have secured justification to intervene regarding various state-led public health and socioeconomic interventions. Accordingly, a series of strong measures would in turn generate a great opportunity to strengthen its public administration capability if it attaches priority to how *smart* it is to protect people's lives and safety, and how *smartly* it can provide public services and support during these difficult times and beyond.

In the new normal era, the concept of competition between nations that has until now been centred on *hard power*, such as the economy and the military, will likely be re-centred on *soft power*, and our COVID-19 experiences may further emphasise that humanity itself becomes the ultimate goal of national security (Szymanski, Smuniewski and Platek, 2020). Effectively managing various newly and potentially redefined national security concepts, including economic security, food security, health security, environmental security, personal security, community security and political security would not be possible without a fully functional smart government systematically underpinned by a broad range of modern technology (Gupta et al., 2021).

With respect to an e-governance system, smart government must be capable of facilitating and supporting better planning and decision-making to provide timely quality public services, with a particular focus on public health and cybersecurity, while the rest of the resources available will have to be invested in enhancing the role of the private sector to bring about innovative technology solutions to improve the smart governance system itself. In doing so, national governments will have to take a leading role in the smart governance solution by taking advantage of its status as a pioneering e-government system.

1.1.2 Control tower for supply chain resilience

The degree of responsiveness to the rapid dynamics of the restructuring of the global supply chain has become a core capability in the COVID-19 era and will be even more so beyond the crisis' end. As the current pandemic is seriously disrupting global and regional value chains, a sizeable number of multinational corporations are expected to take action by reshoring or *U-turning* to their home countries (Hoek, 2020).

According to a survey conducted by the Bank of America (2020), nearly 80 per cent of China-based multinational corporations are currently considering reshoring. In effect, many are exposed to serious damage whereby only one supply chain disruption in the global value chain would destroy their business operations due to being closely linked to a globalised division of labour, from production to sales.

No wonder, in this regard, that reshoring, or at least a plan to repatriate part of production from one country to another, would be encouraged in terms of supply chain system risk management if the pandemic persists. It should, however, be noted that reshoring or the *U-turn* option cannot be considered a fundamental solution capable of mitigating such risks. Diversifying the production bases to reduce labour and transportation costs and maintaining an international division of labour that fits the characteristics of each country and relevant businesses would remain essential in achieving global and regional market competitiveness.

Monitoring such likely dynamic trends associated with supply chain disruption is a particularly critical consideration for a country that has maintained its trade performance by relying heavily on a certain group of countries or regions. Because of this, line ministries and relevant agencies must closely monitor and assess the changing trajectory in the global and regional supply chain. An integrated national approach to quickly respond to such changing dynamics will most probably be the key to future prosperity (Baek, 2019). Hence, the establishment of a nationwide supply chain crisis response centre should be carefully considered. This centre should be fully capable of supply chain resilience planning and management through close cooperation with import/export companies, trade unions, food authorities and a cooperative society. Full digitalisation of all these processes and the cooperation and integration of innovative technology solutions such as blockchain and artificial intelligence (AI) will be required in the months to come (Kalla et al., 2020).

1.1.3 Untact culture and industrial restructuring

Reflecting on our radical experiences over the past months and year, there is an increasing desire to enjoy meals and leisure at home as long as *social distancing* guidelines emphasise that we do so to protect ourselves from COVID-19. We will have to prepare thoroughly for when this so-called *untact* culture is routinised, something that the COVID-19 crisis will most likely leave behind as part of its legacy (Bae and Chang, 2020). In other words, this pandemic is likely to instil in us a perception that a house where one can control everything is the safest place to be. The spread of such an outlook may influence changes in the structure of service sectors, and hence predicting new demands and responding in advance will be crucial for businesses in preparation for new business opportunities. Meanwhile, there would also be an urgent need for governments to prepare preemptive policy alternatives that effectively respond to anticipated industrial restructuring (de Jong and Ho, 2020).

Such prospective restructuring is likely to lead to a new era of *distance education*. This may consist of *blended learning*, which combines online and offline education, or *flipped learning*, in which teachers and students engage in offline discussions after prior online learning (Kocoglu and Tekdal, 2020; Ince, Kabul and Diler, 2020). Such methods are expected to become widespread during and after this crisis. Now is the time for national governments to scale up their efforts to promote these newly emerging education-related business opportunities, in collaboration with various concerned businesses. Furthermore, the government should establish a policy whereby teachers are assigned two clear roles: first, the role of providing *guidance* to help students to progress; and second, the role of *teaching* with an additional function of providing psychological support to students as well (Daniel, 2020; de Filippis, Schmidt and Reza, 2020). Nonetheless, such a policy change and relevant support should consider the feature of public good and address any unequal educational opportunities.

Changes in the ways of working, including video conferencing and telecommuting, are also imperative to consider. Such trends are anticipated to continue, further leading to innovation in terms of office space. *Mobile-based 5G smart office business* may allow most work tasks to be done on a smartphone and may emerge as a new industry or sector. Besides, an emerging business opportunity for *home office* arrangements is likely to bring about huge cost reductions for companies all over the world (Hu, 2020). In other words, a substantial portion of existing large-scale offices may disappear in the post-crisis era.

In responding promptly to the *untact* cultural trend, strengthening the capability to maximise the potential of 5G networks and built-in infrastructure is required (Gupta et al., 2021). In fact, even before this pandemic broke out, many advanced countries had already embraced digitalisation, for example, in the extensive use of online

banking transactions (Seetharaman, 2020). Besides, a large propor-
tion of traditional shopping has already been replaced by online and
mobile shopping. In this context, the current crisis will likely accelerate such banking and shopping trends, among others. Businesses
should thus anticipate this growing trend to capture any foreseeable
opportunities by improving their online transaction capabilities and
platforms.

Underpinning aggregated progress in the developing world, particularly
Africa and Latin America, has been a *grow first and redistribute later*
strategy as a dominant development paradigm,[7] which has left open
questions regarding intra- and inter-generational equity. In Sub-Saharan
Africa, for example, where economic growth has been nearly 3.6 per cent
on average over the period 1990–2020,[8] about 70 per cent of jobs are
considered vulnerable, with youth and women's labour market participation still being very low (ECA et al., 2016). Moreover, extreme poverty
(classified as living on US$1.25 per day or less) decreased by a mere 14
per cent over the period 1990–2012, with 109 million people being added
to the extremely poor group (people living in extreme poverty) during the
same period.[9]

This vulnerability of the labour force, together with persistent levels of
poverty, suggests that much of the benefit of economic growth has been
concentrated within small groups of the population within the above-
mentioned economies. Many households have been compelled to pursue
agricultural businesses, despite declining farm sizes due to rising rural population densities. Meanwhile, Africa has recently experienced a prolonged
era of *de-industrialisation*, which is evidenced by the decline and subsequent stagnation in manufacturing value-added at around 11 per cent of
GDP from 2012, while the service sector's value-added has increased since
2009 (see Figure 1.3).[10]

A dominant economic development school of thought attributes relative
underdevelopment in developing countries to a lack of *structural transformation* or the failure of such countries to significantly transform their
low-productivity agrarian economies into high-productivity industrial ones,
particularly regarding the manufacturing sector.[11] This school emphasises
that structural transformation efforts should target moving away from traditional views of development and make labour-intensive export-led industrialisation a possibility. Accordingly, many African countries have identified
the structural transformation agenda as a development priority in their
national development plans. In fact, many of them have prioritised such an

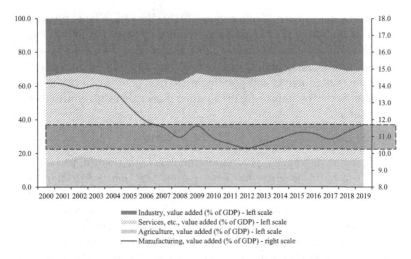

Figure 1.3 Sectoral contributions to GDP in Africa, 2000–2019. Source: Author's own elaboration on the basis of UNCTAD (2021).

agenda in a continental development strategy called Agenda 2063, formulated by the African Union Commission (AUC) (2015).

While structural transformation often lays the foundation for high and sustained economic growth, it is still keenly debated as to whether it can bring about inclusive growth and prosperity for all. This piecemeal approach to dealing with a strategy favouring economic growth that is not sufficiently inclusive could stem largely again from the aforementioned *de-industrialisation* trend, whereby developing economies, particularly African countries, have skipped the transition to manufacturing sector-driven economies and have instead, been transformed to service-sector-driven ones (with lower marginal productivity) (McMillan and Rodrik, 2011). Such a transformation pathway has often been characterised by the fragility and vulnerability associated with informal activities (Nissanke, 2019). In particular, this *abnormal* path of structural transformation coupled with *de-industrialisation* has largely been observed in many parts of Sub-Saharan Africa over the past four decades.

What makes matters worse is that the structural transformation approach is also likely to result in the deterioration of the environment unless concerted action is taken to ensure environmental sustainability (UNCTAD, 2012; Armah and Baek, 2018). According to the World Bank's World Development Indicators (WDI) (2018), the rising rates of greenhouse gas emissions, particularly in Sub-Saharan African countries, have correlated with rising per capita GDP over the past half-century, with a correlation

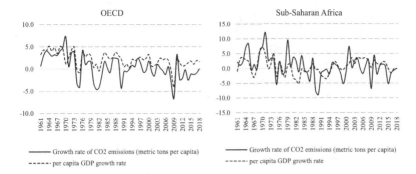

Figure 1.4 The growth trend of carbon dioxide emissions and per capita GDP: OECD versus Sub-Saharan Africa, 1961–2018. Source: Author's own elaboration on the basis of the WDI (2021).

coefficient of 0.475 (see Figure 1.4). This correlation implies that as long as per capita GDP continues to grow, so too will greenhouse gas emissions.

In a more analytical sense, the average growth rate of per capita emissions in member countries of the Organisation for Economic Co-operation and Development (OECD) over the 1980s and 1990s was greater than that of Sub-Saharan African countries, but the trend has completely reversed between the two groups since 2000.[12] It can be interpreted that Sub-Saharan Africa has been able to sustain economic growth over recent years through more radical emissions of carbon dioxide than that of the advanced group. Given the relatively low share of manufacturing contribution to the GDP of many African countries, carbon-driven economic expansion, the early stage of which was rapidly driven by the urbanisation process,[13] has substantially been based on a narrow range of primary commodities, particularly natural resources,[14] including fossil fuels and metallic minerals (Schoneveld and Zoomers, 2015). The current growth pattern in much of Africa may be environmentally unsustainable in this regard.

Structural transformation strategies, while maintaining environmental conservation, are closely associated with the normative idea of sustainable development (Castro, 2004; Hull, 2008). Initially pioneered by the Brundtland Commission, the concept of sustainable development has emerged in relation to recent environmental challenges, prompting a rethink of the development paradigm. Agenda 21, the outcome document from the Earth Summit held in Rio de Janeiro in 1992, called for the integration of environmental and developmental concerns. Subsequently, in 2012, the Rio +20 Conference urged member states of the United Nations (UN) to increase their mainstreaming of sustainable development at all levels (UN,

2012). This normative idea was later institutionalised in 2015, in the 2030 Agenda for Sustainable Development (UN, 2015), which encouraged governments and other actors to address economic, social and environmental sustainability goals simultaneously, and consequently, the synergies and trade-offs between them (Baek, 2018).

The implication of this global normative discourse is that structural transformation should also be pursued in a way that is anchored by its simultaneous effects on the three components of inclusive sustainable development. Integrating pursuit of these two overlapping policy agendas, both aimed at moving away from an exclusive focus on economic growth, raises the following important questions. *What combinations of economic, social and environmental sustainability can feasibly be achieved in the course of structural transformation? How can trade-offs and synergies between economic, social and environmental goals best be incorporated into policy choices?* These are important, practical and complex questions that need addressing in a comprehensive and consistent way. The broad purpose of this book is to contribute towards doing so.

1.2 Research questions

The central objective of the book is to address the following overarching research question.

Overarching question: What is the nature of the relationship between "inclusive sustainable development" and "structural transformation," with particular reference to low-income countries?

The chief principal focus is investigating how efforts to advance the three dimensions of sustainable development affect the process of structural transformation. This part of the research is concerned with scientific observation at the country level through batteries of indicators, with correlations between them being amenable to statistical analysis. For the sake of systematic analysis, this research exercise is divided into the following two separate sub-questions.

Sub-question 1:   How do empirical trade-offs and synergies between economic growth, social inclusion and environmental conservation affect structural transformation outcomes?

Sub-question 2:   What policy measures maximise the synergies to promote structural transformation in line with inclusive sustainable development?

1.3 Scope and methodology

The unit of analysis is set at the national level, and the scope of the book is restricted to the development strategies of low-income countries in the world economy over the next few decades. The performance of these countries remains highly important, not least given the depth and breadth of poverty within them.

Restricting the scope of this research in this way has the analytical advantage that individually they are unlikely to be capable of influencing global policy processes, thus permitting a clear distinction between nationally endogenous and globally exogenous factors, as follows. First, the normative idea of inclusive sustainable development is shaped largely at the global level but considered exogenous to the national level. Second, the regional or meso-level is neglected here as a means by which national and global-level policy processes interact (Haughton and Counsell, 2004). In contrast, Grabel (2017) sheds light on meso-level institutional governance as a source and accelerator of interaction between global and national level policymaking. Third, the time dimension between short-run and long-run is another point to consider. While the normative force of inclusive sustainable development can be considered fully exogenous in the short run, the possibility of it becoming endogenous to the national context increases in longer-term analysis.

As for methodological approach, I employ a mixed method that combines national level theoretical analysis and cross-national level modelling exercises, the results of which are assessed against the overarching framework set in Chapters 2 and 3. The descriptions of the methodological approaches are embedded in the research chapters, covering structural equation modelling techniques (Chapter 4).

1.4 Six development priorities

This section introduces and defines six key terms that are central to this study, these being: (1) *economic growth*; (2) *environmental quality*; (3) *sustainable development*; (4) *inequality reduction*; (5) *inclusive sustainable development*; and (6) *structural transformation*. All these terms are also explained and explored in more depth in Chapters 2 and 3.

The notion of (1) *economic growth* is mostly used to refer to the process by which a country produces more products and services by utilising economic and natural resources in a more efficient manner (Todaro, 2014). In effect, measuring economic growth provides useful information about the size of the quantitative expansion of an economy so as to be able to compare the level and stage of a country's development (Giddings, Hopwood and O'Brien, 2002). GDP (measured by the total cost of goods and services sold in an economy within a year) or gross national income (GNI), especially their per capita terms, are used as the most convenient and objective proxy indicators, becoming the overriding goal of policymaking over the past decades. Yet, the emphasis on efficiency of production often leads to the concentration of capital into the hands of a few capitalists. Such a distorted consequence is invariably accompanied by exacerbating unequal distribution between capitalists and workers unless a timely policy intervention is prioritised. Furthermore, an efficient approach to transforming natural resources into goods and services could also cause a depletion of resources and environmental degradation (Dasgupta, 2013). In particular, the case of natural resources being overused beyond the earth's regenerative capacity could restrain continuous economic activities and production.

Given its potential demerits, the idea of economic growth has radically expanded to take into account several other modern terms (e.g. inclusive growth, equitable growth, sustainable growth) that include concern beyond the material aspects of development.[15] In this regard, the concept of economic growth that is more relevant to the 21st-century context should be understood as economic performance, according to the extent to which the essential needs of people are balanced both socially and economically through the efficient use of natural resources, within ecological limits.[16]

(2) Linking *environmental quality* to economic growth is one proposal initially attempted by the *Club of Rome*,[17] which was concerned with the negative impact of rapid population growth and industrial development under a finite supply of natural resources. This environmental concern was some time later aggravated by Meadows et al. (1972),[18] who warned that if the world's population continued to grow at the current pace, and if industrialisation, the pace of pollution as well as food production practices and the use of resources remained unchanged, the planet would reach its limit for growth within the next 100 years. It was indeed sensational enough not only to lead to national reactions (Furuseth and Cocklin, 1995),[19] it also influenced the global debate over development strategies.

The degree to which environmental considerations impact on the discussion on economic growth strategies greatly depends on how central the environment is to a nation's agenda of socioeconomic development.[20] The Environmental Kuznets Curve (EKC) can bring us some useful insights at this stage (Grossman and Krueger, 1995; López-Menéndez, Pérez and Moreno, 2014). In essence, it explains that higher greenhouse emissions are inevitably accompanied by the industrialisation process, especially in the initial stage of development. Subsequently, curbing such emissions is possible as industrialisation (coupled with an increase in income level and thus, more investment in technology) progresses to advanced technology, particularly in regard to the use of renewable energy. In fact, the level of economic development may not even be so salient nowadays because newly developing countries could decouple large amounts of emissions from their growth process through directly benefitting from various technology transfer mechanisms, including the Technology Facilitation Mechanism[21] and the Technology Bank for the Least Developed Countries.[22]

When these theoretical and practical ideas are endogenised into national policymaking processes, they trigger, through government policies and collective action among individuals and institutions, a country's new change processes that take into account various aspects of environmental quality. As a result of such developments, national initiatives for environmental concerns were institutionalised in the 2015 Paris Agreement that called on all governments to put forward their nationally determined contributions (i.e. reducing carbon emissions) to mitigate and adapt to climate change, potentially contributing to their development process economically and socially, while maintaining the earth's ecological capability.

By conflating the two aforementioned development approaches, (3) the normative idea of *sustainable development* has emerged prominently in the global development discourse. This idea is a contested concept depending on whether the environment is considered as a means or an end to development. From an economic view, Pearce, Barbier and Markandy (1990) held that "sustainable development involves maximising the net benefits of economic development, subject to maintaining the services and quality of natural resources over time," while environmentalists put more emphasis on environmental conservation and protection. Furthermore, Conway and Barbier (1988) viewed it as a human-centred concept, focusing on human capability and progress, arguing that "sustainability is the ability to maintain productivity, whether of a field, farm or nation, in the face of stress or shock." While it is clear from the debates about sustainable development that there is no one single philosophy, it is generally accepted people can have their own interpretation of it (Giddings, Hopwood and O'Brien, 2002). Without a doubt, it must be a much broader concept than merely any single dimension of development. Given this situation, sustainable development may not always be inclusive or equitable.

For sustainable development to be inclusive, effort towards (4) *inequality reduction* is essential.[23] Inequality refers to the extent of variance in the level of a variable across a defined population (e.g. individuals, groups, sectors, nations and regions) and can be applied to multiple dimensions, such as social status, education opportunities, health outcomes or degree of wealth.[24] Notwithstanding the multi-dimensions of inequality, income inequality is the most widely used proxy indicator in measuring the degree of an unequal situation, which is essentially linked to the methodological individualism underpinning neo-classical thinking in capital accumulation.[25] Income inequality largely appears to relate to the process of capital accumulation in economic growth, and hence, to an income measure of development.[26] However, a broader definition needs to be set out in order to adopt more holistic measures of development (Stewart, 2014).

Notably, in his book, *A Theory of Justice* (Rawls, 1971), John Rawls introduced the concept of an acceptable range of wealth and social gap[27] in a society and warned that it would be confronted with social conflict, corruption, bad governance and social movements if the level of social inequality exceeded this range.[28] Equally important is the relation to the environment. Environmental inequality is deeply exposed to the vicious circle of environmental vulnerability that could have a significant impact on the social exclusion or social marginalisation of the poor. For example, the poorest are likely to be the most vulnerable to environmental risks (e.g. various unexpected disasters and polluted areas), whereas the richest are capable of protecting themselves from such risks. Thus, considering environmental inequality in addition to economic and social dimensions is important for capturing the multi-dimensional context of inequality.

By integrating inequality reduction initiatives into the sustainable development concept, I propose it should be named as (5) *inclusive sustainable development*, one that takes into consideration both economic and environmental development in an inclusive fashion. In fact, there is a useful reference point, namely the *triple bottom line*, first coined by John Elkington (2018), an influential scholar who decomposed the normative idea of sustainable development into the social, environmental and economic spheres. This normative concept was institutionalised into 17 SDGs,[29] recognising that global environmental problems must be tackled globally by both the developed and developing world. It also emphasises that an ideal approach to sustainable development is to integrate economic, social and environmental aspects, while also recognising their interlinkages, so as to pursue sustainable development effectively in all its dimensions. In line with such thinking, inclusive sustainable development can be defined as *a long-term development aspiration to guide countries' balanced pursuit of economic prosperity, inclusive growth and environmental sustainability, without compromising the ability of future generations to be able to pursue the same goals.*

The final key term, (6) *structural transformation*, is relatively new development thinking identified by a majority of developing countries (Baek, 2019). This can be defined as a *process* by which the relative importance of different sectors and activities of an economy changes over time.[30] Its central idea focuses on sectoral shifts from agriculture to industry and services, underpinned by differences in inter-sectoral productivity (Elliott, 1998; Herrendorf, Rogerson and Valentinyi, 2013) or such shifts geared by an accelerated process of export diversification and sophistication mainly derived by capability-enhancing factors (Lectard, 2019). Hence, under this lens, it is often assumed that economic growth is a necessary and overriding condition for development. From a more dynamic perspective, it can also be understood in relation to the need for an economy to be flexible enough to effectively adapt its national context to the recent accelerating pace of change in the global environment (Killick, 1995[31]; Hassink, 2010; Hu and Hassink, 2019). In this aspect, structural transformation can accelerate the process of achieving economic sustainability that can be understood not just in terms of "economic growth" but also in that of "increasing resilience" and "reduced volatility" (Nissanke, 2019).

Similar to the concept of sustainable development, its multiple normative features are proving to be obstacles to reaching a clear single consensus on its concrete definition. Each developing country has its own development priority (and different strategies towards structural transformation) given differences in their initial conditions and the status quo of their economy. Incorporating their context-dependent features, many developing countries have already mainstreamed structural transformation aspiration into their national development plans, and these structural transformation measures are monitored and evaluated based on their development outcome framework (CDP, 2018). Recognising such a wide variety of concerns and considerations, structural transformation can be defined both as *a process- and outcome-driven context-dependent national development priority that is utilised for incorporating geographical and sectoral changes in resource allocation, while accommodating for global economic and environmental constraints in a flexible manner.*

1.5 Outline of the book

Chapter 1 is this introductory chapter.

Chapter 2 is designed by tracing the origin of the idea of structural transformation back to the classical development economics literature, and then, there is an exploration as to how this has been expanded over time to incorporate thinking about equity and environmental sustainability.

Chapter 3 contains extensive literature reviews on trade-offs and synergies between (1) economic versus social development, (2) social versus environmental development and (3) environmental versus economic development. This conceptual analysis informs, together with findings from Chapter 2, a rigorous theoretical foundation to address research questions.

Chapters 2 and 3 are thus ultimately designed to provide a consistent overarching framework where a theoretical research goal is attained by synthesising the trinity nexus of economic growth, inequality and environmental sustainability into normative development frameworks, namely the Inclusive Sustainable Development (ISD) framework.

Chapter 4 then benefits from structural equation modelling to empirically investigate their structural effects, such as trade-offs or synergies and how each of the multi-dimensional contributions is transmitted into a structural transformation process, as set in the ISD framework, and provides firm implications in the field of development planning.

Chapter 5 discusses key findings and explains how they are integrated to address the overarching research inquiry, followed by suggestions for further research investigation. Especially in this chapter, a policy simulation is conducted to explore an illustrative way of alternative structural transformation strategies: (1) dirty transformation, (2) green transformation and (3) zero transformation.

Notes

1 According to data from UNCTAD (2021), the aggregated real GDP volume is estimated at US$18 trillion (at constant prices in 2015) for 1970 and US$81 trillion for 2016. On the basis of these two estimated volumes, the size of the world economy has expanded by 448 per cent and the compound annual growth rate is 3.05 per cent over the 50-year period. The same data source is used for the subsequent analysis of developed versus developing economies.

2 For example, Nurkse (1953), Lewis (1954), Solow (1956), Hirschman (1958), Prebisch (1959), Rostow (1960), Kuznets (1973), Romer (1990), Aghion and Bolton (1992), Stiglitz (1996), Sachs (2006), Lin (2012), Piketty (2013) and Milanovic (2016).

3 As there is no one single established convention for the designation of "developed countries" versus "developing countries," this comparative analysis in the introductory chapter is based on UNCTAD's data set and its classification for economic groups.

4 It is resulting in the convergence of the living standards of what some consider to be two different worlds (Korotayev and Zinkina, 2014). This is based on the general assumption that income growth leads to improved living standards. There were, however, a number of exceptions, for instance, despite income growth in India, living standards (as measured by access to toilets or cooking fuel) have not improved much – i.e. the differences between income and multi-dimensional measures of poverty.

5 Like the previous analysis, UNCTAD's classification for economic growth and its data set are applied to this analysis.

6 My policy brief (Baek, 2021) has been posted in the IPR (Institute of Policy Research) blog of the University of Bath. Available from: https://blogs.bath.ac.uk/iprblog/2021/06/24/meta-discourse-on-the-covid-19-crisis-and-beyond.

7 This development paradigm is underpinned by the Kuznets hypothesis that the level of inequality is likely to initially go up as industrialisation takes hold. Detailed theoretical and empirical discussion on this is presented in Chapter 3.

8 Like the previous analysis, UNCTAD's data set is applied.

9 Based on the World Bank's World Development Indicators (2018), in terms of a poverty headcount ratio at US$1.90 per day, this region reduced it by 13 percentage points from 54 per cent to 41 per cent over the period 1990–2014, while the world as a whole registered a reduction of 24 percentage points from 35 per cent to 11 per cent.

10 Although the reverse trend in manufacturing contribution to GDP in Sub-Saharan Africa has been observed since 2012, which is confirmed by an empirical study (Kruse et al., 2021) employing time series of employment and value-added by 12 sectors and in 51 countries for the period 1990–2018, the pace of the recovery appears not enough yet.

11 For example, McMillan and Rodrik (2011), Timmer (2017) and Frankema and van Waijenburg (2018).

12 Averaged 1980–1999 growth rate of per capita greenhouse gas emissions in OECD countries was −0.253, while the growth rate in Sub-Saharan Africa was −1.225, which translates into a 0.625 gap in averaged growth rates between the two groups. However, the figures averaged for 2000–2014 are −0.847 in OECD countries and 0.378 in Sub-Saharan Africa, which implies that OECD countries have reduced their per capita level of emissions, whereas Sub-Saharan African countries have increased theirs (mainly due to their industrialisation efforts). The gap in averaged growth rates since 2000 between the two groups has widened to 1.225. In addition to comparison analysis in terms of per capita greenhouse gas emission, the emission elasticities with respect to economic growth can be calculated for sub-periods and they can further be compared between the two groups. Emission elasticities of economic growth for the period 1961–1999 is 1.47 and 0.32 for OECD countries and Sub-Saharan African countries, respectively, implying that OECD countries have greater responsiveness of their economic growth performance to an increased emission level than that of Sub-Saharan African countries. However, these positive elasticities of both groups turn into negative emission elasticities for the period 2000–2014, which are 0.41 and 0.12, respectively. These elasticity estimations partly support the newly emerged development idea that carbon emissions are no longer effective in deriving the pace of economic growth in the 21st century.

13 "History and experience show that urbanisation and industrialisation are closely associated in a mutually beneficial manner – but not in Africa. African countries must leverage the force of urbanisation to drive and enable industrial development, re-establishing the link between urban growth and industrial growth" said Dr Abdalla Hamdok, Executive Secretary of the UN Economic Commission for Africa in the launch event of the Economic Report on Africa 2017 (ECA, 2017) in New York on 8 December 2017.

14 The relationship between natural resources-rich and economic growth remains highly controversial, especially in the case of Sub-Saharan Africa, where several countries (e.g. Nigeria and the Democratic Republic of Congo) have suffered from the misuse of natural resources, which has hindered economic growth, so-called *resource curse*. Others (e.g. Botswana) have benefitted from the effective use of their natural resources to become upper-middle-income countries (Siegle, 2009).

15 Using per capita GDP remains controversial in terms of reflecting a country's development level or status. For instance, it only provides limited information since going to war increases GDP and destroying infrastructure and re-building it also increases GDP. Partly due to this, there have been proposed a number of

indicators that can address such limitations, e.g. the Genuine Progress Indicator and "Beyond GDP" under the System of Environmental-Economic Accounts.

16 The meaning of "ecological limits" was also postulated by Kate Raworth's (2017) framework of Doughnut Economics, with the terms, "ecological ceilings" or "planetary boundaries."

17 The *Club of Rome* is an organisation of individuals who share a common concern for the future of humanity and strive to make a difference, especially being concerned about the impact of rapid population growth and industrial growth based on a finite supply of resources.

18 Their book, *The Limits to Growth*, shares concerns about the predicament humankind is facing in line with the *Club of Rome*. Immediately after their publication, academics, regardless of their being on the left or right wing of the political spectrum, voiced criticism. Later, the book received fierce criticism from entrepreneurs and even from advocates of capitalism. However, over time, as the environmental challenges have intensified, governments, civil society organisations and even academics have arrived at the affirmative regarding the chief normative claim of the book. Sometime later, an updated revision (Meadows, Randers and Meadows, 2004) was published, which propelled environmental considerations into the centre of the development discourse. In 2008, Graham Turner's (2008) *A Comparison of The Limits to Growth with Thirty Years of Reality* concluded that changes in industrial production, food production and pollution are all in line with the book's predictions of economic and social collapse in the 21st century.

19 For example, strengthened environmental laws, campaigns for legislation on the environment and institutional change through the creation of cabinet-level environmental departments.

20 The socioeconomic development and the environmental quality nexus, for instance, relates to agricultural land, forests and water quality, all of which could have serious implications for other socioeconomic activities. Agricultural land remains a critical endowment that is environmentally sensitive in the sense that environmental conservation policies strictly prohibiting the discharge of industrial waste would lead to more arable land and reduced forest cover compromises the planet's carbon sinks, thus undermining adaptation to climate change (Foody, 2003). Hence, maintaining forest areas is essential for sustaining the earth's ecosystems affecting: the dynamics of species diversity, genetic diversity and biodiversity; and potentially the frequency of floods and drought caused by extreme climate conditions (Zander and Kächele, 1999).

21 The *Technology Facilitation Mechanism* is designed to facilitate multi-stakeholder collaboration and partnerships through the sharing of information, experiences, best practices and policy advice among governments, civil society, the private sector, the scientific community, UN entities and other stakeholders (UN, 2015, para 70).

22 The *Technology Bank for the Least Developed Countries* has been designed to strengthen the knowledge capacity of the least developed countries, thus fostering the development of their national and regional innovation ecosystems (TBLDC, 2017).

23 In May 2019, Bong Joon-ho, the South Korean film director, won a Palme d'Or at the Cannes film festival for his black comic thriller "Parasite." The film is a masterpiece that deals with economic inequality and the gap between the rich and poor in society by sharply contrasting a young, wealthy entrepreneurial

family with a poor family living in a semi-basement. It was effective in gaining sympathy from people around the world, and beyond Korea, even though it portrayed a particular Korean situation represented by the "semi-basement." As such, the problems of economic inequality and polarisation are chronic ills of the modern capitalist society that transcend national borders. The problem is that such polarisation creates a "gap society." As the middle class collapses and the gap between the rich and the poor widens, wealth and poverty are passed down through generations, which robs us of an "equality of opportunity" and kicks the ladder of class mobility. In this ruthless reality, it is the younger generation who are frustrated more than anyone else. As such, the disappointment and frustrations of the young, which should lead to various social pathologies in the years to come, would ultimately inflict a huge loss on national competitiveness.

24 In its multi-dimensional conceptualisation, horizontal inequality (inter-group distribution within countries) and vertical inequality (inequality among individuals within a country) are the focus (Østby, 2008; Cederman, Weidmann and Gleditsch, 2011).

25 This is mainly because income data is relatively easier to access for inequality analysis than other forms. Even the Gini coefficient, which is empirically derived from the Lorenz curve and several other similar measures – e.g. United Nations University World Institute for Development Economics Research (UNU-WIDER), Luxembourg Income Study (LIS) and Standardised World Income Inequality Database (SWIID) – is publicly available for a researcher for comparisons of income inequality across various countries (Solt, 2016).

26 The level of a household's income tends to indirectly correlate, to some extent, with other dimensions of inequality, such as educational attainment, socioeconomic status, political influence, living standards and even the level of happiness (Graham and Felton, 2006).

27 For example, unequal access to education opportunities and difficulties in social mobility.

28 This idea is theoretically mirrored in the so-called *difference principle* – each person is to have an equal right to the most extensive basic liberty compatible with a similar liberty for others.

29 Seventeen Sustainable Development Goals constitute the core of the 2030 Agenda for Sustainable Development.

30 In this book, "structural transformation" is assumed to equate with "structural change" as used by the World Bank or "structural adjustment" as referenced by the International Monetary Fund (IMF). Despite this assumption of the research, it is useful to note that the United Nations uses this term to target the outcome of structural transformation, while the World Bank notes it with more focus on the process and the IMF does focus on the policy interventions.

31 He argues that economies of Eastern Europe and Africa have undergone economic crisis due to their lack of flexibility, while the four Asian Tigers (i.e. Hong Kong, Singapore, South Korea and Taiwan) have structurally transformed their economies owing to their higher adaptability.

References

Aghion, P. and Bolton, P., 1992. Distribution and growth in models of imperfect capital markets. *European Economic Review*, 36(3), pp.603–611.

Armah, B. and Baek, S.J., 2018. Three interventions to foster sustainable transformation in Africa. *Journal of Social, Political and Economic Studies*, 43(1–2), pp.3–25.

AUC (African Union Commission), 2015. Agenda 2063: *The Africa we want. A shared strategic framework for inclusive growth and sustainable development.* Addis Ababa: AUC.

Bae, S.Y. and Chang, P.J., 2020. The effect of coronavirus disease-19 (COVID-19) risk perception on behavioural intention towards "untact" tourism in South Korea during the first wave of the pandemic (March 2020). *Current Issues in Tourism*, 24(7), pp.1017–1035.

Baek, S.J., 2018. *The political economy of neo-modernisation: Rethinking the dynamics of technology, development and inequality.* London: Palgrave Macmillan.

Baek, S.J., 2019. Cooperating in Africa's sustainable structural transformation: Policymaking capacity and the role of emerging economies. *International Development Planning Review*, 41(4), pp.419–434.

Baek, S.J., 2021. *Meta-discourse on the COVID-19 crisis and beyond.* Bath: Institute of Policy Research. Available from: https://blogs.bath.ac.uk/iprblog/2021/06/24/meta-discourse-on-the-covid-19-crisis-and-beyond.

Bank of America, 2020. Global equity strategy: Tectonic shifts in global supply chains. Global research. Available from: https://www.bofaml.com/content/dam/boamlimages/documents/articles/ID20_0147/Tectonic_Shifts_in_Global_Supply_Chains.pdf.

Castro, C.J., 2004. Sustainable development: Mainstream and critical perspectives. *Organization and Environment*, 17(2), pp.195–225.

CDP (Committee for Development Policy), 2018. *Lessons* learned in developing productive capacity: *Fourteen* case studies. New York: UN/DESA (ST/ESA/2018/CDP/37). Available from: https://www.un.org/development/desa/dpad/wp-content/uploads/sites/45/publication/CDP-bp-2017-37.pdf [Accessed 28 February 2020].

Cederman, L.E., Weidmann, N.B. and Gleditsch, K.S., 2011. Horizontal inequalities and ethno-nationalist civil war: A global comparison. *American Political Science Review*, 105(3), pp.478–495.

Conway, G.R., and Barbier, E.B., 1988. After the green revolution: Sustainable and equitable agricultural development. *Futures*, 20(6), pp.651–670.

Daniel, S.J., 2020. Education and the COVID-19 pandemic. *Prospects*, 49, pp.91–96.

Dasgupta, P., 2013. The nature of economic development and the economic development of nature. *Economic and Political Weekly*, 48(51), pp.38–51.

de Filippis, E.M., Schmidt, A.C.S. and Reza, N., 2020. Adapting the educational environment for cardiovascular fellows-in-training during the COVID-19 pandemic. *Journal of the American College of Cardiology*, 75(20), pp.2630–2634.

de Jong, M. and Ho, A.T., 2020. Emerging fiscal health and governance concerns resulting from COVID-19 challenges. *Journal of Public Budgeting, Accounting and Financial Management*, 31(1), pp.1–11.

EBRD (European Bank for Reconstruction and Development), 2020. *Transition report 2020–21: The state strikes back.* London: EBRD.

ECA (Economic Commission for Africa), 2017. *Economic report on Africa 2017: Urbanization and industrialization for Africa's transformation.* Addis Ababa: ECA.

ECA, AUC (African Union Commission), AfDB (African Development Bank) and UNDP (United Nations Development Programme), 2016. *MDGs to Agenda 2063/ SDGs transition report 2016: Towards an integrated and coherent approach to sustainable development in Africa.* Addis Ababa: ECA.

Elkington, J., 2018. 25 years ago I coined the phrase "Triple Bottom Line." Here's why it's time to rethink it. *Harvard Business Review* [Online], Sustainability. Available from: https://hbr.org/2018/06/25-years-ago-i-coined-the-phrase-triple-bottom-line-heres-why-im-giving-up-on-it [Accessed 10 December 2018].

Elliott, D.R., 1998. Does growth cause structural transformation? Evidence from Latin America and the Caribbean. *Journal of Developing Areas*, 32(2), pp.187–198.

Foody, G.M., 2003. Remote sensing of tropical forest environments: Towards the monitoring of environmental resources for sustainable development. *International Journal of Remote Sensing*, 24(20), pp.4035–4046.

Frankema, E. and van Waijenburg, M., 2018. Africa rising? A historical perspective. *African Affairs*, 117(469), pp.543–568.

Furuseth, O. and Cocklin, C., 1995. An institutional framework for sustainable resource management: The New Zealand model. *Natural Resources Journal*, 35(2), pp.243–273.

Giddings, B., Hopwood, B. and O'Brien, G., 2002. Environment, economy and society: Fitting them together into sustainable development. *Sustainable Development*, 10(4), pp.187–196.

Grabel, I., 2017. *When things don't fall apart: Global financial governance and developmental finance in an age of productive incoherence.* Cambridge, MA: MIT Press.

Graham, C. and Felton, A., 2006. Inequality and happiness: Insights from Latin America. *Journal of Economic Inequality*, 4(1), pp.107–122.

Greer, S.L., King, E.J., da Fonseca, E.M. and Peralta-Santos, A., 2020. The comparative politics of COVID-19: The need to understand government responses. *Global Public Health*, 15(9), pp.1413–1416.

Grossman, G.M. and Krueger, A.B., 1995. Economic growth and the environment. *Quarterly Journal of Economics*, 110(2), pp.353–377.

Gupta, D., Bhatt, S., Gupta, M. and Tosun, A.S., 2021. Future smart connected communities to fight COVID-19 outbreak. *Internet of Things*, 13(4), pp.100–342.

Hassink, R., 2010. Regional resilience: A promising concept to explain differences in regional economic adaptability? *Cambridge Journal of Regions, Economy and Society*, 3(1), pp.45–58.

Haughton, G. and Counsell, D., 2004. Regions and sustainable development: Regional planning matters. *Geographical Journal*, 70(2), pp.135–145.

Herrendorf, B., Rogerson, R. and Valentinyi, Á., 2013. Two perspectives on preferences and structural transformation. *American Economic Review*, 103(7), pp.2752–2789.

Hirschman, A.O., 1958. *The strategy of economic development.* New Haven, CT: Yale University Press.

Hoek, R.V., 2020. Research opportunities for a more resilient post-COVID-19 supply chain: Closing the gap between research findings and industry practice. *International Journal of Operations & Production Management*, 40(4), pp.341–355.

Hu, R., 2020. COVID-19, smart work, and collaborative space: A crisis-opportunity perspective. *Journal of Urban Management*, 9(3), pp.276–280.

Hu, X. and Hassink, R., 2019. Adaptation, adaptability and regional economic resilience: A conceptual framework. In: G. Bristow and A. Healy, eds. *Handbook on regional resilience*. London: Edward Elgar.

Hull, Z., 2008. Sustainable development: Premises, understanding and prospects. *Sustainable Development*, 16(2), pp.73–80.

Ince, E.Y., Kabul, A. and Diler, I., 2020. Distance education in higher education in the COVID-19 pandemic process: A case of Isparta Applied Sciences University. *International Journal of Technology in Education and Science*, 4(4), pp.343–351.

Kalla, A., Hewa, T., Mishra, R.A., Ylianttila, M. and Liyanage, M., 2020. The role of blockchain to fight against COVID-19. *IEEE Engineering Management Review*, 48(3), pp.85–96.

Killick, T., 1995. *The flexible economy: Causes and consequences of the adaptability of national economies*. London: Routledge.

Kocoglu, E. and Tekdal, D., 2020. Analysis of distance education activities conducted during COVID-19 pandemic. *Educational Research and Reviews*, 15(9), pp.536–543.

Korotayev, A. and Zinkina, J., 2014. On the structure of the present-day convergence. *Campus-Wide Information Systems*, 31(2/3), pp.139–152.

Kruse, H., Mensah, E., Sen, K. and de Vries, G., 2021. *A manufacturing renaissance? Industrialization trends in the developing world*. WIDER Working Paper 28/2021. Available from: https://www.wider.unu.edu/sites/default/files/Publications/Working-paper/PDF/wp2021-28-manufacturing-renaissance-industrialization-trends-developing-world.pdf.

Kuznets, S., 1973. Modern economic growth: Findings and reflections. *American Economic Review*, 63(3), pp.247–258.

Lectard, P., 2019. Sustainable structural change in the context of global value chains. In: C. Monga and J.Y. Lin, eds. *The Oxford Handbook of Structural Transformation*. Oxford: Oxford University Press.

Lewis, W.A., 1954. Economic development with unlimited supplies of labour. *Manchester School*, 22(2), pp.139–191.

Lin, J.Y., 2012. *New structural economics: A framework for rethinking development and policy*. Washington, DC: World Bank Publications. Available from: http://siteresources.worldbank.org/DEC/Resources/84797-1104785060319/598886-1104951889260/NSE-Book.pdf.

López-Menéndez, A.J., Pérez, R. and Moreno, B., 2014. Environmental costs and renewable energy: Re-visiting the environmental Kuznets curve. *Journal of Environmental Management*, 145(1), pp.368–373.

Maddison, A., 2008. Shares of the rich and the rest in the world economy: Income divergence between nations, 1820–2030. *Asian Economic Policy Review*, 3(1), pp.67–82.

McMillan, M. and Rodrik, D., 2011. Globalization, structural change and productivity growth. In: M. Bachetta and M. Jansen, eds. *Making globalization socially sustainable*. Geneva: World Trade Organization, pp.49–84.

Meadows, D.H., Meadows, D.L., Randers, J. and Behrens III, W.W., 1972. *The limits to growth*. New York: Universe Books.

Meadows, D.H., Randers, J. and Meadows, D.L., 2004. *Limits to Growth: The 30-year update*. Vermont: Chelsea Green Publishing.

Milanovic, B., 2016. *Global inequality: A new approach for the age of globalization*. Cambridge: Harvard University Press.

Nissanke, M., 2019. Exploring macroeconomic frameworks conducive to structural transformation of sub-Saharan African economies. *Structural Change and Economic Dynamics*, 48, pp.103–116.

Nurkse, R., 1953. *Problems of capital formation in underdeveloped countries*. Oxford: Oxford University Press.

Østby, G., 2008. Polarization, horizontal inequalities and violent civil conflict. *Journal of Peace Research*, 45(2), pp.143–162.

Parente, S., 2001. The failure of endogenous growth. *Knowledge, Technology and Policy*, 13(4), pp.49–58.

Pearce, D.W., Barbier, E.B. and Markandy, A., 1990. *Sustainable development: Economics and environment in the third world*. London: Edward Elgar.

Piketty, T., 2013. *Capital in the twenty-first century*. Cambridge: Harvard University Press.

Prebisch, R., 1959. Commercial policy in under-developed countries. *American Economic Review*, 49(2), pp.251–273.

Rawls, J., 1971. *A theory of justice*. Cambridge: Harvard University Press.

Raworth, K., 2017. *Doughnut economics: Seven ways to think like a 21st-century economist*. Vermont: Chelsea Green Publishing.

Romer, P.M., 1990. Endogenous technological change. *Journal of Political Economy*, 98(5), pp.71–102.

Rostow, W.W., 1960. *The stages of economic growth: A non-communist Manifesto*. Cambridge: Cambridge University Press.

Sachs, J.D., 2006. *The end of poverty: Economic possibilities for our time*. New York: Penguin.

Sachs, J.D., and A.M. Warner., 1997. Fundamental sources of long-run growth. *American Economic Review*, 87(2), pp.184–188.

Schoneveld, G. and Zoomers, A., 2015. Natural resource privatisation in Sub-Saharan Africa and the challenges for inclusive green growth. *International Development Planning Review*, 37(1), pp.95–118.

Seetharaman, P., 2020. Business models shifts: Impact of Covid-19. *International Journal of Information Management*, 54, pp.102–173.

Siegle, J., 2009. Governance strategies to remedy the natural resource curse. *International Social Science Journal*, 57(s1), pp.45–55.

Solow, R.M., 1956. A contribution to the theory of economic growth. *Quarterly Journal of Economics*, 70(1), pp.65–94.

Solt, F., 2016. The standardized world income inequality database. *Social Science Quarterly*, 97(5), pp.1267–1281.

Stewart, F., 2014. Sustainability and inequality. *Development*, 57(3–4), pp.344–361.

Stiglitz, J.E., 1996. Some lessons from the East Asian miracle. *World Bank Research Observer*, 11(2), pp.151–177.

Szymanski, F.M., Smuniewski, C. and Platek, A.E., 2020. Will the COVID-19 pandemic change national security and healthcare in the spectrum of cardiovascular disease? *Current Problems in Cardiology*, 45(9), pp.100645.

TBLDC (Technology Bank for the Least Developed Countries), 2017. *Report on the work of the Technology Bank for the Least Developed Countries in 2017.* New York: TBLDC (TBLDC/2017/4/Rev.1). Available from: http://unohrlls.org /custom-content/uploads/2018/03/TBLDC-2017-4-Rev1-EN.pdf [Accessed 3 March 2018].

Timmer, C.P., 2017. Food security, structural transformation, markets and government policy. *Asia & the Pacific Policy Studies*, 4(1), pp.4–19.

Todaro, M.P., 2014. *Economic development.* 12th ed. (The Pearson Series in Economics). Philadelphia, PA: Trans-Atlantic Publications.

Turner, G.M., 2008. A comparison of the limits to growth with 30 years of reality. *Global Environmental Change*, 18(3), pp.397–411.

UN (United Nations), 2012. *The future we want. Resolution adopted by the General Assembly on 27 July 2012.* New York: UN (A/RES/66/288).

UN, 2015. *Transforming our world: The 2030 Agenda for Sustainable Development.* New York: UN.

UNCTAD (United Nations Conference on Trade and Development), 2012. *Economic development in Africa Report 2012: Structural transformation and sustainable development in Africa.* Geneva: UNCTAD.

UNCTAD, 2021. *UNCTADstat* [Online]. Geneva: UNCTAD. Available from: http:// unctadstat.unctad.org [Accessed 10 September 2021].

World Bank, 2018. *World development indicators* [Online]. Washington, DC: World Bank. Available from: http://data.worldbank.org/data-catalog/world -development-indicators [Accessed 11 June 2018].

World Bank, 2021. *World development indicators* [Online]. Washington, DC: World Bank. Available from: http://data.worldbank.org/data-catalog/world -development-indicators [Accessed 10 September 2021].

Zander, P. and Kächele, H., 1999. Modelling multiple objectives of land use for sustainable development. *Agricultural Systems*, 59(3), pp.311–325.

2 Revisiting the theoretical foundation of structural transformation towards sustainability

2.1 Precursors to structural transformation theory

Traditional notions of structural transformation emphasise sectoral shifts from agriculture to industry and services. While there is broad consensus that structural transformation is associated with economic growth and development, there has been considerable debate about the drivers of such transformation. Therefore, understanding the significance of reshaping *economic structure and sectoral composition* should be placed at the core of my overarching framework. However, this entails systematically addressing the theoretical foundation of a country's development process (or "modernising economic system"), which inevitably calls for tracing the origin of the idea of structural transformation back to the classical development economics literature.

Eight decades ago, Fisher (1939) and Clark (1940) cast light on a particular pattern of national development and postulated it as a transformation paradigm, whereby as the economy advances, the major production activity shifts from primary (i.e. the extraction of raw materials through agriculture, fishing, forestry and mining sectors) to secondary (i.e. industrial production through manufacturing and construction sectors) and then, finally, to tertiary (i.e. the provision of education and tourism services). One of the early users of the term, *structural transformation*, Simon Kuznets (1955) cited it as one of the six central characteristics in the process of modern economic growth when observing how certain patterns regarding the reallocation of economic activity across agricultural, manufacturing and services sectors naturally take place. Since then, structural transformation has often been equated with a *modernisation process* (Islam and Iversen, 2018).

Arthur Lewis (1954) articulated such processes differently. He particularly focused on the structural shift of the labour force between sectors and named it the *dual-sector* pattern. According to his model, agricultural and industrial sectors generally coexist when an economy undergoes

DOI: 10.4324/9781003259916-2

rapid industrial development through benefitting from low-cost farming. However, as the rural labour force continues to flow into the cities, certain challenges arise there when the labour force from the rural area becomes exhausted, thus reaching a *turning point*.[1] A structure comprising high cost, but low efficiency, then becomes deeply embedded in a society, thereby resulting in a slowdown in economic growth. Lewisian thought was consistent with various traditional schools of thought, including Rosenstein-Rodan (1943), Prebisch (1950)[2], Nurkse (1953), Singer (1953), Murphy, and Shleifer and Vishny (1989), among others.[3]

Of the many prior works, Hirschman (1958) is worth revisiting in terms of thinking of structural transformation as a dual-sector process. In his version, so-called *unbalanced dual-sector* growth, he introduced the concept of forwards and backwards linkages where the former linkage is created through investment in a project that encourages another investment in subsequent stages of production, while the latter one is realised when a project itself encourages investment in facilities that enables the project for success. Based on such linkage dynamics, he claimed that those projects that can best create linkages should be the ones for massive investment consideration. In other words, a special effort to foster a particular industry (or sector) has to be made, because it could create a leading industry that generates a chain reaction for other industries, termed the *domino effect*. He elaborated it based on a positive circulating process repeated by *lead* versus *pull* between industries. This circulating pattern will intensify a chain of interactions between *leading* and *chasing* sectors and will, thus, raise the level of industrial competitiveness. Since then, this *unbalanced sector* model[4] has become dominant in structural transformation modelling.

For instance, Baumol (1967) incorporated two sectors of *progressive* versus *non-progressive* interactions with a particular consideration of the effect of technological changes. His propositions stated that labour productivity increases cumulatively at a compounded rate of growth in the *progressive* sector, while in the *non-progressive* one its rate is constant. From his modelling exercise, he concluded that sustaining balanced growth in the reality of an unbalanced productivity trend would result in zero economic growth. This modelling result clearly indicates that sectoral productivity should be continuously balanced, depending on a country's stage of transformation. This could further reflect that managing trade-offs between sectors is an essential area of policymaking, where inclusive and/or equitable policy interventions come into effect.

A similar policy implication can also be derived from the modelling exercise undertaken by Matsuyama (1992), who focused his attention on the role of agricultural productivity. He hypothesised that (1) income elasticity of demand in the agricultural sector is less than unitary, (2) labour productivity in the industrial sector increases largely driven by *learning-by-doing* externalities[5] and (3) that productivity in the agricultural sector was exogenous to his model. The empirical findings supported a negative relationship between agricultural productivity and economic growth, and hence, allocating more labour force to the manufacturing sector (rather than agricultural) tends to accelerate the pace of economic growth.

In more recent years, modelling a transition process with a particular focus on industrialisation from the agricultural to the manufacturing sector has become predominant. Park (1998), for instance, endogenised factors (e.g. land, unskilled labour force and capital stock) as well as goods (e.g. agricultural, manufacturing and new capital goods) in one model, and stressed the crucial role of the size of the capital-producing sector for economic growth. Various studies with similar emphasis on the role of the manufacturing industry as an engine of economic growth (while also emphasising the importance of an increase in agricultural sector productivity) have been conducted but with a different focus on what catalyses such a role, for example, the household saving rate (Laitner, 2000) or different income elasticities of demand across sectors (Caselli and Coleman, 2001). These *unbalanced* pattern modellers were able to provide empirical evidence that sectoral contributions to GDP vary across sectors. This is why the pace of economic growth also varies by country, and hence, the importance of country-specific sectoral analysis and looking at it in particular in terms of cross-sector growth rates and trade-offs cannot be overestimated.

2.2 More recent structural transformation theories

In recent years, a new wave of modelling structural transformation has emerged by incorporating services into the theory.[6] Kongsamut, Rebelo and Xie (2001), for instance, attempted to build a *three-sector framework*, in which structural transformation is driven by income effects while assuming the real interest rate remains constant. With a similar framework, Ngai and Pissarides (2007) applied to their model the concept of the growth rates of *sectoral total factor productivity* as a driving force of structural transformation. They found the convergence of employment into two sector types, those producing capital goods and those generating the lowest rate of growth in productivity. Its long-run simulation predicted that the share of the agricultural sector is decreased and that the share of the manufacturing sector is increased at first and then declines later, while the services employment share increases.

A study conducted by Foellmi and Zweimüller (2008) also supported such a sectoral shifts phenomenon. These researchers assumed hierarchical preferences on the demand side, meaning that households tend to consume according to a hierarchy of needs (hierarchy function), which character-ises their willingness to shift from high priority to low priority products and vice versa. Within their theoretical modelling framework that adopts Engel's consumption cycle,[7] they found that the rich are likely to demand newly invented products, while the poor tend to only consume necessities. However, as income grows, the poor start demanding more luxuries, induc-ing a market shift towards product innovation. As their modelling simulation continues, the results firmly confirmed the *agricultural-manufacturing-services sector* transition. This modelling that focuses on sectoral differ-ences in income elasticities of demand could eventually reach the broad consensus that structural transformation is a continuous process via sectoral shifts from agriculture to industry and services, essentially claimed by the studies focusing on sectoral differences in productivity growth (Duarte and Restuccia, 2010; Ungor, 2017; Timmer, 2017[8]).

Despite its theoretical and empirical value, the agricultural-manufac-turing-services sector transition advocates may, however, be exposed to a critical limitation, especially when the 21st-century context is taken into account. The bulk of the models reviewed have focused on endogenous interactions within a country, thereby elaborating the structural transfor-mation process within a relatively closed economy. Often, the sectoral transition has been forced by external factors other than the outgrowth of industrial development dynamics developed internally. This oversight may be partly due to, on the one hand, for the sake of simplicity in their model-ling exercise, or on the other, in relation to the time of the development of their sectoral models (the global economy was considered "closed" in the mid-to-late 20th century).

Especially the latter point would be serious given the fact that in the 21st century the structural transformation process must have been accompa-nied by aggressive globalisation forces, possibly resulting in an unexpected direction of transformation. Unlike the past transformative trajectory that most developed countries underwent, the experiences of, for instance, many African countries have been associated with agriculture to the service-sec-tor transition, as the emergence of newly invented technology goods and services has been robust since 2000, as a result of globalisation. This has created differences in the potential expansion of demand, particularly in the high-tech services industry and sectors, inducing somewhat distorted secto-ral transition in many of these countries.

It is however critical to differentiate between a sectoral transition dynamic to the high-tech productivity services sector and a transition to the services sector largely characterised by the fragility and vulnerability associated with informal activities. The former transition can be considered a contributing factor to productivity-enhancing structural transformation, whereas the latter one could affect the pattern of productivity-reducing structural transformation, which has historically been observed in many parts of Sub-Saharan Africa over the past four decades (Nissanke, 2019). Integrating these different transition dynamics to their urbanisation discourse, Gollin, Jedwab and Vollrath (2016) attempted to differentiate between the two different processes of urbanisation: (1) urbanisation to "production cities" where manufacturing sector activities play a key role in industrialising cities; and (2) urbanisation to "consumption cities" where non-tradable services are dominating cities' activities. Observing a sample of 116 developing countries over the period 1960–2010, they concluded that the urbanisation process to the consumption cities tends to be prevalent among countries whose economies are heavily dependent on natural resource exports. This result is also consistent with the development trajectory largely characterised by the productivity-reducing transformation in developing countries, particularly Sub-Saharan Africa.

In short, factors distorting the structural transformation process can be summarised as follows. The rapid pace of globalisation has, indeed, increased competition in the consumer products and services market and also enabled flows of capital and human resources without borders.[9] It has, thus, let some countries benefit from cheap resources (e.g. labour force), thereby increasing their productivity and fostering sectoral shifts in an efficient fashion, while a completely opposite state of affairs has been the case for others (Mills, 2009; Guidetti, 2014). Moreover, globalisation can also intensify societal relations, which link distant localities so that some economic events in rural areas can be significantly influenced by events that occur in other areas or even in other countries (Giddens, 1991). This implies reciprocal influences of certain tendencies and simultaneously a localisation or urbanisation process, which may deviate from the traditional pathway of structural transformation.

2.3 Calls for sustainable structural transformation

In a globalised world, the integration of the economy with social, cultural and environmental structures raises strong concerns on the environmental sustainability of structural transformation. In essence, the global community is increasingly demanding that the transformation process (sectoral transition) be environmentally sustainable. Understanding such a *global call* should, however, entail exploring how an idea of structural transformation incorporating the concerns of sustainability has developed over time (see Box 2.1[10]).

BOX 2.1   COOPERATING FOR AFRICA: TWO CHALLENGES TO MEETING DEVELOPMENT GOALS

Currently, Africa faces a great challenge in that the considerable development objectives that the continent must meet are being tackled through addressing two separate agendas. At the regional level, Africa has its own long-term development framework – Agenda 2063 – that aims to achieve an integrated, prosperous and peaceful Africa. Then, at the global level, the 2030 Agenda for Sustainable Development – adopted in September 2015 – sets out Sustainable Development Goals (SDGs) that are comprehensive and promise to rally global partners in support of Africa's development.

Under these two agendas, Africa is now confronted with a dual transition: the global-level transition from the Millennium Development Goals (MDGs) to the SDGs, and the continent-wide implementation of Agenda 2063. The numbers of goals, targets and indicators involved in each plan reflect just how complex this dual transition is: Agenda 2063 has seven aspirations, 20 goals and 34 priority areas, 171 national targets, 85 continental targets and approximately 246 indicators, while the SDGs comprise 17 goals, 169 targets and 230 indicators. Implementation will be no easy task for African countries.

These two agendas will provide a foundation for Africa's inclusive growth and structural transformation. To achieve this, both African countries and development partners need to scale up their commitments to the implementation of the plans by leveraging synergies among them (Baek, 2018). Two factors are critical in this regard: engagement on Africa's part with emerging partners, and a commitment from Africa and its partners to prioritise KID – knowing, integrating and domesticating both agendas – to make its goals achievable.

2.1.1 Africa's engagement with development partners

The first area to be addressed is emerging partnerships, which will provide the financial framework within which development agendas can be achieved. Undoubtedly, global partnerships have been playing an important role in Africa's development during the MDG implementation era through bridging financing gaps for development and building policymaking and technology capacities. There is, however, still a considerable gap in addressing the special needs of African countries – such as the promotion of inter- and intra-continental trade, infrastructure development and governance improvement as well as environmental management. The most effective channel of such partnerships is trade, which has been a major commitment from development partners. Recent World Trade Organization international trade statistical analysis, however, indicates that the share of Africa's exports in the global market has continuously declined since 2012 when it stood at 2.7 per cent in 2012, at 2.6 per cent in 2014 and 2.3 per cent in 2016 (Baek, 2019). This is partly due to unfavourable movement in global commodity prices, which have a significant impact on investment and economic growth in Africa, given its heavy dependence on natural resource products for export.

Another essential channel is official development assistance or ODA. Based on analysis of OECD development statistics, Africa has maintained its position as the largest recipient of ODA over the past three decades, meaning that almost half of world ODA was injected into Africa (Armah and Baek, 2015). It should be noted, however, that most OECD-DAC countries do not meet their ODA commitments to provide 0.7 per cent of their countries' GNI. In fact, the total ODA from the DAC group reached only 0.29 per cent of the combined GNI – implying a delivery gap of 0.41 per cent. Because this huge gap is unlikely to narrow in the near future, the quality of ODA and its use have to be seriously taken into consideration.

2.1.2 Role of emerging economies in Africa's development

In the light of these global partnership trends, there are a number of action points for both Africa and development partners. First of all, it is imperative that African governments strengthen macroeconomic sustainability and public management of natural resource revenues and leverage such funds for the transformation of their economies.

Given the substantial delivery gap in ODA commitments, it is also extremely important for Africa to develop and strengthen part-nerships with emerging economies such as BRICS (Brazil-Russia-India-China-South Africa) as an alternative, but also very important, sources of financing, learning and technology. For instance, accord-ing to Oxfam International's Africa-China Dialogue Platform (Gore,

2015), China has emerged as the largest trading partner to Africa over the past five years: Africa's trade volume with China reached US$225 billion, which is twice that the continent shares with the United States. Furthermore, Chinese foreign direct investment and other forms of development assistance to Africa are substantially increasing.

With this growing role of emerging partners, in addition to that of traditional development partners, the international community together should work closely with African governments to strengthen capacities for domestic resource mobilisation and particularly to curb illicit financial outflows. According to the ECA's study (2015) on illicit financial flows, Africa is currently losing more than US$50bn annually – almost double the foreign aid flowing into Africa – from aggressive tax avoidance practices by multinational companies.

2.1.3 Africa's dual transition to the SDGs and Agenda 2063

The second point to which I refer is the dual transition that Africa must undertake to address both the SDGs and Agenda 2063. Despite the challenges identified above, recent developments at the regional and global levels point to an increasingly supportive financial environment for Africa. The question now is: what are the challenges associated with dual transition, and which areas of development should both Africa and development partners focus on and how? For this, the *MDGs to Agenda 2063/SDGs Transition Report 2016* clearly identified challenges and opportunities.

The implementation of both agendas requires advocacy for and sensitisation to the details of both frameworks to ensure awareness of their mutual relevance to national development and the relationship and synergies between them (SDSN, 2018). In this context, the 2030 Agenda for Sustainable Development should be understood as an attempt to respond to the global dimensions of Africa's development challenges, while Agenda 2063 should be viewed as a response to continent-specific development challenges and aspirations, many of which overlap.

With the sheer volume of goals, targets and indicators embodied in each of the agendas, there is inevitably significant convergence between them. In this regard, an integrated set of goals, targets and indicators – along with a harmonised review and reporting platform to develop a core set of continental indicators – is required to effectively track progress on both agendas. Such arrangements need to take into account the levels of development of individual countries (Willis, 2016). While convergence between the two agendas is significant, integrated and coherent implementation of both agendas into national planning systems will be an operational challenge as significant as it is vital.

2.1.4 Capacity matters most

In effect, successful implementation requires strengthened capacities for policymaking and the analysis of inter- and intra-sectoral impacts of policy initiatives. Even with the adoption of the SDGs alone, countries will require an integrated approach that simultaneously addresses the economic, social and environmental dimensions of sustainability in a balanced way. This is an area where evidence-based analysis of the structural effects (trade-offs and synergies) of key policies is needed (Baek, 2017; 2018).

In the past there has been a tendency to consider immediate benefits above all else; the economic benefits of increased oil production, for example, were not adequately weighed against the possible negative environmental and social costs. Therefore, there should be a significant effort to identify the most appropriate institutional architecture that individual countries can use to facilitate the effective implementation of the two agendas. Invariably, the role of planning agencies will be paramount in ensuring that the economic, social and environmental dimensions of policy decisions are reflected in a balanced manner in all aspects of programme and project execution (Armah and Baek, 2018).

In this new age of Africa's development, multi-stakeholder partnerships remain one of the most critical means of mobilising internal and external resources. Furthermore, the active participation of emerging partners is required to address Africa's challenges of dual transition and to support its operationalisation. In this regard, traditional partners and emerging nations need to establish ways of partnering and cooperating with each other towards supporting Africa in realising its development aspiration, particularly for the areas of KID:

- *[K]nowing about both agendas* to simultaneously address the three dimensions of sustainability with strengthened evidence-based policymaking capacities

- *[I]ntegrating both agendas* to harmonise frameworks and establish common mechanisms of implementation and follow-up architecture
- *[D]omesticating both agendas* in national planning frameworks with strengthened institutional capacities for effective institutional coordination and arrangements

Reflected in the Environmental Kuznets Curve (EKC), the notion of *grow first and clean up later* has been prevalent in past decades (Baek, 2019). Radical economic transformation actually led to a drop in the unemployment rate and to material abundance, a benefit that was considered to overwhelm concern about environmental degradation from a substantial increase in carbon emissions. As a result, most countries were convinced that there would be "no problem" regarding resource depletion. This was largely influenced by the work of the *unlimitedness* advocates, who were mostly growth-oriented scholars with the belief that the Earth would overcome its limitations by some means or other and that, for instance, resource depletion and environmental degradation (exogenous to their growth models) could be resolved by technological advances.[11] They believed that even the challenges of non-renewable resources (related to climate change) and food shortages could be settled by the natural effect of diffusion of alternative energy innovation.[12]

On the other hand, the *limitedness* advocates, initiated by the *Club of Rome*, warned that if the world's population continued to grow at the current pace, and if industrialisation, the pace of pollution, food production practices and the use of resources remained unchanged, the planet would reach its limit for growth within the next 100 years. While admitting the possibility that technological advances may prolong this end point, they insisted that technology could not be the fundamental solution. Turner (2008), for instance, claimed that even three to four decades after the most influential book in this doctrine, *The Limits to Growth*, was first released, the trend analysis adopted in the book was still valid since the level of environmental pollution and ozone depletion, as warned, continue to be massively challenging issues today.

With these global environmental challenges, humanity needed to rethink the traditional development paradigm and the concept of sustainable development emerged as a result (Hull, 2008). Under this lens, greater environmental considerations in addition to economic and social interests in the development process are demanded. Now, it has become a concept that is comparable to democracy and globalisation, which is found everywhere

(Castro, 2004). In essence, it is widely perceived that global environmental problems must be tackled by the developed and developing world together.[13] For instance, advanced countries seem already on track in terms of structural transformation, but their continuous transformation process in a sustained fashion remains uncertain. For them in this regard, sustainable development appears to be not merely a desired goal of development, but rather, a prerequisite for their competitive and continuous transformation process (Langhelle, 2000).

Meanwhile, developing countries could be attracted by being able to set their own development directions in line with their own environmental and geographical conditions. African countries, for instance, could take geographical advantage in producing renewable energies given their vast untapped water resources and abundant sunshine (Collier and Venables, 2012; Simon, 2013). In addition, fragile economies, particularly those of Arab countries, could also benefit from the sustainable development initiative as it calls for good governance and strengthened global and regional cooperation to stabilise geopolitical tensions (such as worsening refugee crises and shaky investor confidence) (ESCWA, 2018). As for both developed and developing countries, this global goal could assist them in utilising their environmental resources efficiently to contribute to their own transformation processes and reinforcing their taking responsibility for the environmental challenges, with the overall aim of enhancing their international standing by making policy in a self-conscious manner.

Against this background, the normative concept of structural transformation is now being changed to focus on: pursuing more than the material aspects of life (i.e. beyond economic growth); innovating the process of schooling and allocating human capital;[14] and incorporating the environment at the centre of production and consumption patterns. In particular, the capacity of accommodating uncertainties[15] has also become an additional element of the normative concept (Killick, 1995; Hassink, 2010; Hu and Hassink, 2019). The work of Killick deserves a revisit, for instance. He elaborated that structural transformation is defined in relation to the need for an economy with a flexible structure in order to be adaptable. This definition was empirically supported by the cases in which the economies of Eastern Europe and Africa have undergone economic crisis due to their lack of flexibility, while the four Asian Tigers (i.e. Hong Kong, Singapore, South Korea and Taiwan) have structurally transformed their economies owing to their higher adaptability. This role can be further mainstreamed into a policymaking capacity to transform. The stance of policymakers should be flexible enough to anticipate and then accelerate structural transformation through: (i) removing any of newly emerging obstacles that would block the needed changes in the sectoral structure of the economy; and (ii) adapting in a timely manner to the changing imbalance in the allocation in human capital between urban and rural areas.

2.4 Structural transformation, sustainability versus social inclusion

In the light of this *global call* for sustainability to be placed at the centre of policymaking, the importance of a normative idea of sustainable development to be integrated into a country's structural transformation process can be recognised. A large number of scholars, however, remain concerned about potential conflict (compatibility) between reality and the normative aspect. Mindful of this, in this section, there is an assessment as to whether structural transformation can be an initiative that provides greater space to encompass environmental conservation, social inclusion and the interaction of the multi-dimensions of sustainable development. In this regard, addressing the following three interrelated concerns should be a prerequisite: *Do the efforts to advance the process of structural transformation necessarily bring economic growth? Do these efforts inevitably cause social problems, such as a widening of inequality?* and *Is the process of structural transformation necessarily correlated with the destruction of the environment?*

With respect to the first concern, there is broad agreement among scholars that structural transformation defined according to a two- or three-sector model is positively related to economic growth.[16] This doctrine explains that structural transformation stimulates growth by reallocating resources from low- to high-productivity activities. Other scholars have also suggested that the manufacturing sector promotes growth because it embodies technology and innovation, which fuel the productivity and development process (Shen, Dunn and Shen, 2007, UNCTAD, 2018). The alternative view is that export-led development strategies on the principle of comparative advantage stimulate growth, which could over time cause structural transformation by accelerating transition out of agriculture into industry and services (Swiecki, 2017; Teignier, 2018).

The empirical studies conducted on this relationship have, however, yielded mixed results. For instance, structural transformation in South Korea has been associated with the role of international trade in accelerating the transition from agriculture to industry and services (Sposi, 2019). Also, Ungor (2017) found that differences in sectoral productivity growth rates accounted for the different sectoral reallocations in Latin America and East Asia. Moreover, Cortuk and Singh (2011) assessed this relationship in India for the period 1951–2007, employing the Granger causality test, and they found that from 1988 onwards, there was a significant positive impact from structural transformation to growth. Their empirical results strongly support the general consensus that Indian radical economic growth observed over the last two decades has been a result of such transformation processes. However, other studies using Granger causality analysis have found that the causal relationship is country-specific, implying that there may be no universal relationship between the two variables (Elliott, 1998; Mijiyawa, 2017[17]). The second concern is also at the heart of the social development discourse over the past decades.

It is, indeed, still debated as to whether the structural transformation process can bring about social development, with a particular focus on inequality and human development. In reality, unfortunately, the transformation process is not always accompanied by inclusive growth and prosperity for all, but rather, it often coexists with rising inequalities and a slower-than-anticipated pace of poverty reduction (ECA et al., 2016). This is partly because transformation is mainly concerned with the reallocation of economic activities towards higher productivity sectors and not a pro-poor growth intervention that is associated with increasing incomes and employment opportunities for the poorer segments of the population.[18] Hence, it is not always the case that a sectoral shift to the productive sector benefits the lower end of the distribution (Caliendo et al., 2018). Of course, there is a possibility to link them (social development and structural transformation) together towards positive results of both – for example, doubling efforts to reduce the skills gap in human capital in order to match the skills required in both the agricultural and higher productivity sectors.

Empirically, a large number of studies have suggested that the development outcomes depend on the nature of the transformation. For instance, Dastidar (2012) found that where structural transformation was characterised by a transition from agriculture to industry, inequality levels did not increase in developing countries. On the other hand, inequality was found to increase in those developing countries experiencing an agriculture-service transformation. In the latter case, the increase in inequality was more pronounced when the initial levels of inequality are already higher than average. This argument can be supported by a logic developed by Nurkse (1953) claiming that the level of inequality influences the size and composition of the aggregate demand, often thereby reducing the market for manufacturing production, assuming that importing of manufactured goods remains unchanged. In a similar vein, more recently, scholars have highlighted the misallocation and underutilisation of resources as outcomes of inequality that could delay the transformation process (Restuccia and Rogerson, 2017).

Last but not least, environmental concern in the process of structural transformation has to sit at the forefront of the public policy agenda (UN,

2021a). However, the theoretical evidence on the environmental drivers of structural transformation is scant compared with that of the above economic and social drivers. Nevertheless, the EKC would appear to provide some insights on this concern. According to it, industrial transformation initially causes higher emissions of greenhouse gases (mostly in the case of developing countries); however, net emissions eventually drop (mostly in the case of developed countries) as the increase in income level leads to technological advancements associated with curbing such emissions. Its empirical validity, however, depends on the environmental good in question,[19] although many empirical studies appear to support this perspective.[20]

On the other hand, the *green growth* advocates[21] have rejected the story of developing countries argued by those of the EKC. Instead, they have absorbed the insight in the case of developed countries and then applied the case to developing countries too. Simply speaking, their central argument is that with current technological innovations, newly developing countries can decouple greenhouse gas emissions from their transformation processes. The past experiences of Norway and Sweden suggest that countries can achieve high levels of human development while attaining low levels of per capita carbon dioxide emissions (Bhattacharjee and Iftikhar, 2011). Other studies (e.g. Collier and Venables, 2012; Simon, 2013; UNEP, 2015) have further claimed that, relative to other continents, the potential for greening the economy is highest in Africa. This is based on the assumption that Africa would willingly jump from fossil fuels to green energy if it were to benefit from the diffusion of green technology. This would put the continent in a position to leverage synergies between environmental quality and structural transformation. In fact, some African countries, including Ethiopia, are already among the global frontrunners in this area.

These views have also been mirrored in empirical accounts. Several researchers (Ladislaw, Leed and Walton, 2014; Alfredsson et al., 2018) have contended that structural transformation strategies under a *business-as-usual* scenario would leave a considerable environmental footprint, which would inversely hinder continuous transformative activities. Naudé (2011) attributed such environmental degradation to a country's carbon-intensive process of structural transformation while proposing environmental-friendly strategies that focus on transferring labour away from environmentally harmful agricultural industries. The role of foreign direct investment (FDI) for environmental conservation was also studied by Zhang and Zhou (2016). Using China's provincial panel data, they found mixed results as to whether FDI-driven transformation reduces emission levels, whereas unequivocal evidence was found that urbanisation programmes radically increase levels. In this context, most of the recent research efforts[22] have increasingly come out against the *de-growth* policy option (Levallois, 2010) or traditional views on trade-offs between the environment and structural transformation, instead, being aimed at exploring the potential synergy effects.[23]

Indeed, the aforementioned three potential tensions could stem from the distinction of the two normative agendas between structural transformation and sustainable development: the idea that structural transformation tends to focus on technical standpoints of sectoral compositional change of output and/or employment within national boundaries, whereas the sustainable development idea goes beyond such a sectoral perspective by taking into consideration multi-dimensions of the national development process in an open economy. While these two could share some commonality in that both are aimed at moving away from an exclusive focus on economic growth, they also reinforce the responsibility of all relevant stakeholders to integrate both agendas into national development plans. The responsible actors are, therefore, able to develop pathways effectively through which structural transformation can be best achieved while balancing potential trade-offs and synergies between economic growth, social inclusion and environmental conservation. In this context, realising these potential synergies would greatly be conditioned by balancing country change processes, which can be effective in reconciling holistically these two development objectives into one unified process of sustainable structural transformation. Such a holistic development idea can play a role in downgrading the aforementioned three potential tensions and make them rather imaginary.

Notes

1 This is the transitioning moment, namely, the *Lewisian turning point*, where society passes through a turning point of the labour force from the status of *excess* to *shortage* or, in other words, structural discrepancy between the demand and supply of the labour market is associated with a sharp rise in wages.

2 Prebisch and Singer are notably structuralist theorists who attempted to explore the structure of production as the fundamental problem in impeding autonomous industrialisation and also emphasise the importance of human capital for increasing returns to investment, while concerning international dualism, which would result in uneven technological progress in the centre and periphery according to their dependency theory.

3 The *big-push* pattern, initially advocated by Paul Rosenstein-Rodan (1943) and advanced further by Murphy, Shleifer and Vishny (1989) and most recently emphasised by Nissanke (2019), is worth revisiting. This pattern's advocates assert that a significant amount of investment, particularly in the early phase of a country's development, should be made in a rapid and timely manner to deal with the persistent poverty level of developing countries. During a similar period, another influential thinker was Ragnar Nurkse (1953), who introduced the theory of the *vicious circle of poverty*. According to this model, the lack of capacity for capital formation in underdeveloped countries leads to a higher

poverty rate, which, in turn, can lead to challenges for effective capital formation. This bi-directional causality can be explored through three channels: high interdependence between income and capital; causality between poverty and health; and close linkages between poverty and education. As per his argument, the vicious circle of poverty would perpetuate the poverty level of developing countries and thus, how to stem this vicious circle becomes a fundamental challenge for these countries. Despite these influential ideas, coordination failure among various industrial policies or complementary activities cannot be underestimated. Unless massive and coordinated policy efforts supported by the optimal allocation of resources are accompanied, it often leads to market failure that could cause poverty traps, particularly in the least developed countries (Glavan, 2008).

4 The *unbalanced* school of thought was initiated notably by Hirschman's model (1958) and Baumol (1967), being later followed by Matsuyama (1992), Park (1998), Laitner (2000), Caselli and Coleman (2001) and Gollin, Parente and Rogerson (2002), among others.

5 Matsuyama's model neglects the existence of a learning-by-doing effect on the agricultural sector, and thus, his analysis fails to incorporate the impact of technological progress on agricultural productivity.

6 For example, Kongsamut, Rebelo and Xie (2001), Ngai and Pissarides (2007), Foellmi and Zweimüeller (2008), Acemoglu and Guerrieri (2008) and Boppart (2014)

7 The introduction of new goods is integrated in the sense that starts with luxury ones with high-income elasticity and ends with necessities with low-income elasticity.

8 Marcel P. Timmer invoked a broader definition as being composed of the following features: relative decline of low-productivity agriculture and low value-added extractive activities; a relative increase in manufacturing and high-productivity services; a decline in the relative share of agricultural employment in the GDP; a rural-to-urban migration that stimulates the process of urbanisation; and the rise of a modern industrial and service economy.

9 For instance, Araujo and Lima (2007) explore the connection between sectoral composition in trade and the difference in income elasticities of demand. This approach is based on Multi-Sectoral Thirlwall's law, which states that the equilibrium growth rate corresponds to the ratio between its income elasticity of demand for exports and that of imports, multiplied by the growth rate of external demand (Romero and McCombie, 2016). The empirical result from Araujo and Lima's research is that the rate of economic growth can be accelerated through shifts in the sectoral composition of trade dynamics. In line with this central idea, Araujo (2013) further advances modelling specification by endogenising technical change and insisting that a country producing final goods with higher income elasticity of demand would result in higher technological advancements and thus, faster economic growth than one producing goods with a lower elasticity of demand.

10 My policy brief (Baek, 2016) has been posted in the IPR (Institute of Policy Research) blog of the University of Bath. Available from: https://blogs.bath.ac.uk/iprblog/2016/10/25/cooperating-for-africa-two-challenges-to-meeting-development-goals.

11 For example, Myers and Simon (1994), Jorgenson and Stiroh (2000), Lomborg (2001) and Hanson (2008).

12 We are now living in a society in which technological innovation (information and knowledge) can spread within minutes all across the world. Thus, diffusion of technology has firmly entered the arena of policymaking. This diffusion can help an individual country prepare strategy or policy that is relevant to its present socioeconomic conditions. Most sensationally, futurist Ray Kurzweil (2005) popularised the idea of technological singularity. In his book, he argues that through the law of accelerating returns, technology is progressing towards a singularity to create superintelligence. In this regard, this school of thought seems to believe that "there is no impossibility" on the basis that technology will bring us more than we can currently imagine.

13 Today, the hegemony of global economic development has already shifted from the Global North (responsible for 40 per cent of global GDP) to the Global South (nearly 60 per cent of GDP). Such a shift would appear to have also been reflected in the competing discourse of Ecological Modernisation versus Sustainable Development. According to the World Bank's World Development Indicator (2018), Western-Advanced Nations constitute about 40 per cent of global GDP: the United States with 24.3 per cent; Germany with 4.5 per cent; the United Kingdom with 3.9 per cent; France with 3.2 per cent, Italy with 2.4 per cent; Spain with 1.6 per cent; the Netherlands with 1.0 per cent; and others with less than 1.0 per cent. While Non-Western-Advanced Nations represent about 60 per cent of global GDP: China with 14.8 per cent; India with 2.8 per cent; Brazil with 2.4 per cent; South Korea with 1.9 per cent; Mexico with 1.5 per cent; and others.

14 Through this process innovation, national human capital is accumulated in a way that drives the differences in the rate of technical progress. Doing so will, in turn, shape sector-specific strengths, thereby inducing structural transformation (UN, 2021b).

15 The uncertainties can be related to power shifts, economic growth, social development, differentiation and specialisation as well as adaptability to a new environment.

16 For example, Lewis (1954), Hirschman (1958), Kuznets (1973), Chenery and Syrquin (1975) and Herrendorf, Rogerson and Valentinyi (2013).

17 A cross-country analysis of 53 African countries found a U-shaped relationship between income growth and the manufacturing sector's contribution to GDP. The increase in per capita GDP is accompanied by a decrease in the manufacturing share of GDP until a threshold of US$943 (current value), while beyond this level incomes are positively associated with the manufacturing sector's contribution to GDP.

18 While sectoral transition from agriculture directly to services could make the African experience unique, the job-creating effect, especially for the poor from this prevailing transition, has been relatively limited, as the manufacturing sector has the greater potential for employment creation.

19 For instance, while carbon dioxide emissions hardly declined with levels of development, sulphur dioxide emissions diminished by 74 per cent among EU countries due to factors such as fuel-switching to low-sulphur fuels, including natural gas and the impact of EU directives relating to the sulphur content of certain other fuels (Armah and Baek, 2018).

20 Empirical support the EKC – e.g. Pao and Tsai (2010), Arouri et al. (2012), Hamit-Haggar (2012), Saboori and Sulaiman (2013), Al-mulali et al. (2013) and Kivyiro and Arminen (2014).

No empirical evidence of the EKC – e.g. Luzzati and Orsini (2009), Iwata, Okada and Samreth (2012) and Onafowora and Owoye (2014).

21 The United Nations Environment Programme (UNEP), a front runner for this greening strategy advocacy, defined green growth as "growth in income and employment should be driven by public and private investments that reduce carbon emissions and pollution, enhance energy and resource efficiency, and prevent the loss of biodiversity and ecosystem services" (UNEP, 2011, p.16).

22 On similar lines, while recent empirical findings have so far supported the theoretical hypothesis of trade-offs between transformation and environmental degradation, they have also highlighted the mediating role of policy in this relationship. For instance, the work of Moscona (2018) centred on the role of the Green Revolution in influencing transformation through increases in agricultural productivity in India and found empirical evidence that such increased productivity drives growth in income and employment in the agricultural sector but impedes the urbanisation process and employment growth in the manufacturing sector.

23 The traditional transformational process (i.e. Western-centric development strategies) is often accompanied by a depletion of resources and environmental degradation (Hamilton and Clemens, 1999; Dasgupta, 2013).

References

Acemoglu, D. and Guerrieri, V., 2008. Capital deepening and non-balanced economic growth. *Journal of Political Economy*, 116(3), pp.467–498.

Al-mulali, U., Lee, Y.M.J., Mohammed, A.H. and Sheau-Ting, L., 2013. Examining the link between energy consumption, carbon dioxide emission, and economic growth in Latin America and the Caribbean. *Renewable and Sustainable Energy Reviews*, 26, pp.42–48.

Alfredsson, E., Bengtsson, M., Brown, H.S., Isenhour, C., Lorek, S., Stevis, D. and Vergragt, P., 2018. Why achieving the Paris agreement requires reduced overall consumption and production? *Sustainability: Science, Practice and Policy*, 14(1), pp. 1–5.

Araujo, R., 2013. Cumulative causation in a structural economic dynamic approach to economic growth and uneven development. *Structural Change and Economic Dynamics*, 24, pp.130–140.

Araujo, R. and Lima, G., 2007. A structural economic dynamics approach to balance-of-payments-constrained growth. *Cambridge Journal of Economics*, 31(5), pp.755–774.

Armah, B. and Baek, S.J., 2015. Can the SDGs promote structural transformation in Africa? An empirical analysis. *Development*, 58(4), pp.473–491.

Armah, B. and Baek, S.J., 2018. Three interventions to foster sustainable transformation in Africa. *Journal of Social, Political and Economic Studies*, 43(1–2), pp.3–25.

Arouri, M.H., Ben Youssef, A., M'henni, H. and Rault, C., 2012. Energy consumption, economic growth and CO2 emissions in Middle East and North African countries. *Energy Policy*, 45, pp.342–349.

Baek, S.J., 2016. Cooperating for Africa: Two challenges to meeting development goals. Bath: Institute of Policy Research. Available from: https://blogs.bath

.ac.uk/iprblog/2016/10/25/cooperating-for-africa-two-challenges-to-meeting
-development-goals.

Baek, S.J., 2017. Is rising income inequality far from inevitable during structural transformation? A proposal for an augmented inequality dynamics. *Journal of Economics and Political Economy*, 4(3), pp.224–237.

Baek, S.J., 2018. *The political economy of neo-modernisation: Rethinking the dynamics of technology, development and inequality*. London: Palgrave Macmillan.

Baek, S.J., 2019. Cooperating in Africa's sustainable structural transformation: Policymaking capacity and the role of emerging economies. *International Development Planning Review*, 41(4), pp.419–434.

Baumol, W.J., 1967. Macroeconomics of unbalanced growth: The anatomy of urban crisis. *American Economic Review*, 57(3), pp.415–426.

Bhattacharjee, S. and Iftikhar, U.A., 2011. *Greening human development: Capturing wins in equity and environmental sustainability*. UNDP Human Development Report.

Boppart, T., 2014. Structural change and the Kaldor facts in a growth model with relative price effects and non-Gorman preferences. *Econometrica*, 82(6), pp.2167–2196.

Caliendo, L., Parro, F., Rossi-Hansberg, E. and Sarte, P., 2018. The impact of regional and sectoral productivity changes on the U.S. economy. *Review of Economic Studies*, 85(4), pp.2042–2096.

Caselli, F. and Coleman, J., 2001. The U.S. structural transformation and regional convergence: A reinterpretation. *Journal of Political Economy*, 109(3), pp.584–616.

Castro, C.J., 2004. Sustainable development: Mainstream and critical perspectives. *Organization and Environment*, 17(2), pp.195–225.

Chenery, H.B. and Syrquin, M., 1975. *Patterns of development: 1950–1970*. London: Oxford University Press.

Clark, C., 1940. *The conditions of economic progress*. London: McMillan and Co.

Collier, P. and Venables, A.J., 2012. Greening Africa? Technologies, endowments and the latecomer effect. *Energy Economics*, 34(S1), pp.S75–S84.

Cortuk, O. and Singh, N., 2011. Structural change and growth in India. *Economics Letters*, 110(3), pp.178–181.

Dasgupta, P., 2013. The nature of economic development and the economic development of nature. *Economic and Political Weekly*, 48(51), pp.38–51.

Dastidar, A.G., 2012. Income distribution and structural transformation: Empirical evidence from developed and developing countries. *Seoul Journal of Economics*, 25(1), pp.25–52.

Duarte, M. and Restuccia, D., 2010. The role of the structural transformation in aggregate productivity. *Quarterly Journal of Economics*, 125(1), pp.129–173.

ECA (Economic Commission for Africa), 2015. *Illicit financial flows (report to the high-level panel on illicit financial flows from Africa)*, Addis Ababa: ECA.

ECA, AUC (African Union Commission), AfDB (African Development Bank) and UNDP (United Nations Development Programme), 2016. *MDGs to agenda 2063/ SDGs transition report 2016: Towards an integrated and coherent approach to sustainable development in Africa*. Addis Ababa: ECA.

Elliott, D.R., 1998. Does growth cause structural transformation? Evidence from Latin America and the Caribbean. *Journal of Developing Areas*, 32(2), pp.187–198.

ESCWA (Economic and Social Commission for Western Asia), 2018. *Survey of economic and social developments in the Arab region 2017–2018*. Beirut: ESCWA.

Fisher, A.G.B., 1939. Primary, secondary and tertiary production. *Economic Record*, 15(1), pp.24–38.

Foellmi, R. and Zweimüller, J., 2008. Structural change, Engel's consumption cycles and Kaldor's facts of economic growth. *Journal of Monetary Economics*, 55(7), pp.1317–1328.

Giddens, A., 1991. *The consequences of modernity*. Palo Alto, CA: Stanford University Press.

Glavan, B., 2008. Coordination economics, poverty traps, and the market process: A new case for industrial policy? *The Independent Review*, 13(2), pp.225–243.

Gollin, D., Parente, S. and Rogerson, R., 2002. The role of agriculture in development. *American Economic Review*, 92(2), pp.160–164.

Gollin, D., Jedwab, R. and Vollrath, D., 2016. Urbanization with and without industrialization. *Journal of Economic Growth*, 21(1), pp.35–70.

Gore, T., 2015. *Extreme carbon inequality: Why the Paris climate deal must put the poorest, lowest emitting and most vulnerable people first*. Oxford: Oxfam International.

Guidetti, R., 2014. Theoretical approaches to inequality in economics and sociology. *Transcience*, 5(1), pp.1–15.

Hamilton, K. and Clemens, M., 1999. Genuine savings rates in developing countries. *World Bank Economic Review*, 13(2), pp.333–356.

Hamit-Haggar, M., 2012. Greenhouse gas emissions, energy consumption and economic growth: A panel cointegration analysis from Canadian industrial sector perspective. *Energy Economics*, 34(1), pp.358–364.

Hanson, R., 2008. Economics of the singularity. *IEEE Spectrum*, 45(6), pp.37–42.

Hassink, R., 2010. Regional resilience: A promising concept to explain differences in regional economic adaptability? *Cambridge Journal of Regions, Economy and Society*, 3(1), pp.45–58.

Herrendorf, B., Rogerson, R. and Valentinyi, Á., 2013. Two perspectives on preferences and structural transformation. *American Economic Review*, 103(7), pp.2752–2789.

Hirschman, A.O., 1958. *The strategy of economic development*. New Haven, CT: Yale University Press.

Hu, X. and Hassink, R., 2019. Adaptation, adaptability and regional economic resilience: A conceptual framework. In: G. Bristow and A. Healy, eds. *Handbook on Regional Resilience*. London: Edward Elgar.

Hull, Z., 2008. Sustainable development: Premises, understanding and prospects. *Sustainable Development*, 16(2), pp.73–80.

Islam, S.N. and Iversen, K., 2018. *From "structural change" to "transformative change": Rationale and implications*. New York: UN/DESA (ST/ESA/2018/DWP/15). Available from: https://www.un.org/esa/desa/papers/2018/wp155_2018.pdf [Accessed 11 January 2019].

Iwata, H., Okada, K. and Samreth, S., 2012. Empirical study on the determinants of CO2 emissions: Evidence from OECD countries. *Applied Economics*, 44(27), pp.3513–3519.

Jorgenson, D.W. and Stiroh, K.J., 2000. Raising the speed limit: U.S. economic growth in the information age. *Brookings Papers on Economic Activity*, 31(1), pp.125–235.

Killick, T., 1995. *The flexible economy: Causes and consequences of the adaptability of national economies*. London: Routledge.

Kivyiro, P. and Arminen, H., 2014. Carbon dioxide emissions, energy consumption, economic growth, and foreign direct investment: Causality analysis for sub-Saharan Africa. *Energy*, 74, pp.595–606.

Kongsamut, P., Rebelo, S. and Xie, D., 2001. Beyond balanced growth. *Review of Economic Studies*, 68(4), pp.869–882.

Kurzweil, R., 2005. *The singularity is near: When humans transcend biology*. New York: Penguin.

Kuznets, S., 1955. Economic growth and income inequality. *American Economic Review*, 45(1), pp.1–28.

Kuznets, S., 1973. Modern economic growth: Findings and reflections. *American Economic Review*, 63(3), pp.247–258.

Ladislaw, S.O., Leed, M. and Walton, M.A., 2014. *New energy, new geopolitics*. Washington, DC: CSIS.

Laitner, J., 2000. Structural change and economic growth. *Review of Economic Studies*, 67(3), pp.545–561.

Langhelle, O., 2000. Sustainable development and social justice: Expanding the Rawlsian framework of global justice. *Environmental Values*, 9(3), pp.127–152.

Levallois, C., 2010. Can de-growth be considered a policy option? A historical note on Nicholas Georgescu-Roegen and the Club of Rome. *Ecological Economics*, 69(11), pp.2271–2278.

Lewis, W.A., 1954. Economic development with unlimited supplies of labour. *Manchester School*, 22(2), pp.139–191.

Lomborg, B., 2001. *The skeptical environmentalist: Measuring the real state of the world*. Cambridge: Cambridge University Press.

Luzzati, T. and Orsini, M., 2009. Natural environment and economic growth: Looking for the energy-EKC. *Energy*, 34(3), pp.291–300.

Matsuyama, K., 1992. Agricultural productivity, comparative advantage, and economic growth. *Journal of Economic Theory*, 58(2), pp.317–334.

Mijiyawa, A.G., 2017. Drivers of structural transformation: The case of the manufacturing sector in Africa. *World Development*, 99, pp.141–159.

Mills, M., 2009. Globalization and inequality. *European Sociological Review*, 25(1), pp.1–8.

Moscona, J., 2018. *Agricultural development and structural change within and across countries*. MIT Department of Economics Working Paper. Available from: http://economics.mit.edu/files/13482.

Murphy, K.M., Shleifer, A. and Vishny, R.W., 1989. Industrialization and the big push. *Journal of Political Economy*, 97(5), pp.1003–1026.

Myers, N. and Simon, J., 1994. *Scarcity or abundance: A debate on the environment.* New York: Norton.

Naudé, W., 2011. Climate change and industrial policy. *Sustainability,* 3(7), pp.1003–1021.

Ngai, L.R. and Pissarides, C.A., 2007. Structural change in a multisector model of growth. *American Economic Review,* 97(1), pp.429–443.

Nissanke, M., 2019. Exploring macroeconomic frameworks conducive to structural transformation of sub-Saharan African economies. *Structural Change and Economic Dynamics,* 48, pp.103–116.

Nurkse, R., 1953. *Problems of capital formation in underdeveloped countries.* New York: Oxford University Press.

Onafowora, O.A. and Owoye, O., 2014. Bounds testing approach to analysis of the environment Kuznets curve hypothesis. *Energy Economics,* 44, pp.47–62.

Pao, H.T. and Tsai, C.M., 2010. CO2 emissions, energy consumption and economic growth in BRIC countries. *Energy Policy,* 38, pp.7850–7860.

Park, S., 1998. Transitional dynamics of structural changes. *Seoul Journal of Economics,* 11(1), pp.75–99.

Prebisch, R., 1950. *The economic development of Latin America and its principal problems.* New York: UN.

Restuccia, D. and Rogerson, R., 2017. The causes and costs of misallocation. *Journal of Economic Perspectives,* 31(3), pp.151–174.

Romero, J.P. and McCombie, J., 2016. The multi-sectoral Thirlwall's law: Evidence from 14 developed European countries using product-level data. *International Review of Applied Economics,* 30(3), pp.301–325.

Rosenstein-Rodan, P., 1943. Problems of industrialization of Eastern and South-Eastern Europe. *Economic Journal,* 53(210/211), pp.202–211.

Saboori, B. and Sulaiman, J., 2013. Environmental degradation, economic growth and energy consumption: Evidence of the Environmental Kuznets Curve in Malaysia. *Energy Policy,* 60, pp.892–905.

SDSN (Sustainable Development Solutions Network), 2018. *Africa SDG index and dashboard report 2018.* Kigali and New York: The Sustainable Development Goals Centre for Africa and SDSN.

Shen, J., Dunn, D. and Shen, Y., 2007. Challenges facing U.S. manufacturing and strategies. *Journal of Industrial Technology,* 23(2), pp.2–10.

Simon, D., 2013. Climate and environmental change and the potential for greening African cities. *Local Economy,* 28(2), pp.203–217.

Singer, H., 1953. Obstacles to economic development. *Social Research,* 20(1), pp.19–31.

Sposi, M., 2019. Evolving comparative advantage, sectoral linkages, and structural change. *Journal of Monetary Economics,* 103, pp.75–87.

Swiecki, T., 2017. Determinants of structural change. *Review of Economic Dynamics,* 24(1), pp.95–131.

Teignier, M., 2018. The role of trade in structural transformation. *Journal of Development Economics,* 130, pp.45–65.

Timmer, C.P., 2017. Food security, structural transformation, markets and government policy. *Asia & the Pacific Policy Studies,* 4(1), pp.4–19.

Turner, G.M., 2008. A comparison of The Limits to Growth with 30 years of reality. *Global Environmental Change*, 18(3), pp.397–411.

UN (United Nations), 2021a. *Exploring climate action in Kuwait: A focus on environmentally sustainable finance*. Kuwait: UN. Available from: https://kuwait.un.org/en/download/76508/142240 [Accessed 10 September 2021].

UN, 2021b. *Unlocking human capital potential in Kuwait as Global Actor in the Knowledge Economy*. Kuwait: UN. Available from: https://kuwait.un.org/en/download/76503/134060 [Accessed 10 September 2021].

UNCTAD (United Nations Conference on Trade and Development), 2018. *The least developed countries report 2018: Entrepreneurship for structural transformation: Beyond business as usual*. Geneva: UNCTAD.

UNEP (United Nations Environment Programme), 2011. *Towards a green economy: Pathways to sustainable development and poverty eradication: A synthesis for policy makers*. Nairobi: UNEP.

UNEP, 2015. *Building inclusive green economies in Africa: Experience and lessons learned 2010–2015*. Nairobi: UNEP.

Ungor, M., 2017. Productivity growth and labor reallocation: Latin America versus East Asia. *Review of Economic Dynamics*, 24, pp.25–42.

Willis, K., 2016. Viewpoint: International development planning and the sustainable development goals (SDGs). *International Development Planning Review*, 38(2), 105–111.

World Bank, 2018. *World development indicators* [Online]. Washington, DC: World Bank. Available from: http://data.worldbank.org/data-catalog/world-development-indicators [Accessed 11 June 2018].

Zhang, C. and Zhou, X., 2016. Does foreign direct investment lead to lower CO_2 emissions? Evidence from a regional analysis in China. *Renewable and Sustainable Energy Reviews*, 58, pp.943–951.

3 An integrated framework for sustainable structural transformation

3.1 The Inclusive Sustainable Development framework

This section introduces the key components and their interactions, as conceptualised in the Inclusive Sustainable Development (ISD) framework (see Figure 3.1), with accompanying discussion on its limitations.

Normative frameworks adopted by national governments to inform country-specific development strategies are presented in Box 1, including: (a) a process- and outcome-driven context-dependent development framework that is utilised for incorporating geographical and sectoral changes in resource allocation, while accommodating for global economic and environmental constraints in a flexible manner; and (b) a long-term development aspiration to guide countries' balanced pursuit of economic prosperity, inclusive growth and environmental sustainability without compromising the ability of future generations to be able to pursue the same goals. These two normative frameworks provide a range of development strategic options to national governments (depending on their development priorities and national contexts). These two development objectives could further be reconciled/embedded into the one unified process of structural transformation that is both inclusive and sustainable (Nissanke, 2019) as the two objectives are presented with a dashed line.

Systematic interactions take place between normative frameworks and country change processes (Box 3), which are defined as the specific processes of (c) economic, (d) social and (e) environmental change, measured through three sets of indicators: economic growth, income inequality and environmental quality, i.e. (f) Box 1↔Box 2. This interaction is materialised through institutions and influential individuals. Meanwhile, the normative frameworks are, of course, influenced by exogenous drivers of change (Box 3), including (g) global debates on development strategies, (h) global process of technological change and (i) initial socioeconomic

DOI: 10.4324/9781003259916-3

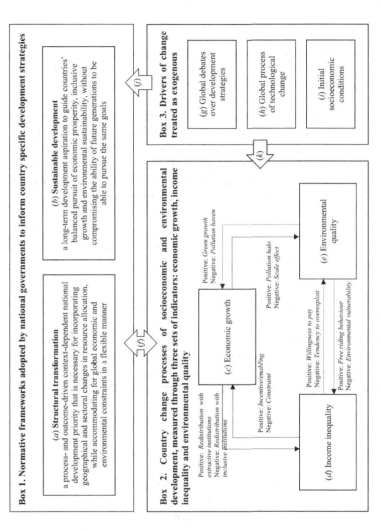

Figure 3.1 The Inclusive Sustainable Development (ISD) framework.

conditions, i.e. (j) Box 3→Box 1. Exogenous drivers of change also influence country change processes, i.e. (k) Box 3→Box 2. Global debates are, however, not significantly affected by change processes nor the normative development framework of individual countries or governments of (small) low- or middle-income countries. Hence, arrows flow out from Box 3, but not into it.

Yet, a limitation of my exclusive focus on the two normative ideas is that it may not reflect comprehensive policy dynamics, and hence, the work needs to be extended to address the challenges of: balancing macroeconomic stability with structural transformation (Nissanke, 2019); mainstreaming the three dimensions of sustainable development into national planning frameworks (Fischer et al., 2015); and mutually reinforcing the role of institutions in supporting sustainable transformation (Osman, Alexiou and Tsaliki, 2012), among others. Furthermore, there are additional areas that could be worth revisiting in line with the ISD framework. That is, the regional intervention on the national development framework. This could be a quite important area because regional intervention would not only affect the linking up of national policies with the normative goals around sustainable development and structural transformation and vice versa, for it would also speed up the process of interactions between the national and global dimensions (Haughton and Counsell, 2004; Grabel, 2017).[1]

Furthermore, the ISD framework assumes the technological effect for country change processes to be exogenous, reflecting most cases for low-income countries, where technological advancement is likely to be adopted from outside a country's borders, rather than being developed during their own country's change processes. Nonetheless, assuming the role of technological progress as an exogenous variable may not be the case for some low-income countries, for example, Ethiopia becomes one of the global frontrunners in clean technology (UNEP, 2015). Given such an outlier case, the initial set scope of study may restrain the ISD framework's explanatory power on the complex dynamics in play. However, endogenising it into the framework would render empirical work far more complex (even impossible).

Overall, filling all these gaps to advance the ISD framework is worthy of study, but they are beyond the scope of the present study. It should also be recognised that such research would be built upon a completely different set of literature compared with that covered in this work. Sticking to the initial scope of analysis for this book allows for the focus to be on my chief aim of informing a broad concept of inclusive sustainable development during the process of structural transformation in a developing country context.

3.2 Dynamics over country change processes

This section explores country change processes of socioeconomic and environmental development in relation to internal dynamics that could reinforce sustainable development more inclusively (Box 2 of Figure 3.1).

Understanding such change processes is critical as this could play an active role in filtering out development areas that seem not to be salient to national priorities, while simultaneously contributing to the formulation of national strategies. In this regard, this section focuses on the empirical grounds for country change processes, primarily concerned with scientific observation through batteries of indicators, with the correlations between them being amenable to statistical analysis.

There is a useful reference in this regard, namely the *triple bottom line*, first coined by John Elkington (2018), who contextualises the normative idea of sustainable development into the social, environmental and economic value. Referring to this, I wish to examine a three-dimensional concept, combining indicators of economic growth, income inequality and environmental sustainability with their trade-offs and synergy effects. Specifically, three potentially interacted areas (trinity nexus) in country change processes are: (i) *economic growth* versus *inequality*; (ii) *inequality* versus *environmental quality*; and (iii) *environmental quality* versus *economic growth*. The existing relevant literature on these is summarised in Table 3.1.

3.2.1 Economic growth versus inequality

In connection with the first nexus in country change processes, the seminal work of Simon Kuznets (1955) needs to be revisited. His hypothesis was that there is an inverse relationship between economic growth and inequality, which became known as the *inverted U-shaped curve* or simply *Kuznets curve*. He argued that inequality is likely to increase initially as industrialisation takes hold. These change processes are driven by the transfer of labour from the low-wage, low-inequality agricultural sector to a relatively high-wage, high-inequality, industrial sector. This hypothesis, however, remains controversial,[2] which largely stems from two reasons: the existence of four competing schools of thought is one; and the other is related to the different views on the direction of causality running from inequality to economic growth, or vice versa. These two in question are important as they are greatly influencing the basis for policymakers to target effective redistribution of wealth to promote economic growth: *trickle-down* versus *trickle-up* oriented interventions or other policy options.[3]

Table 3.1 Literature review on bi-directional causality for the economic growth–inequality–environmental quality nexus

Causality	From inequality to economic growth	From economic growth to inequality
Positive	*Incentive hypothesis*: Income inequality provides incentives for more effort in order to gain more, thereby contributing to an engagement in a wide range of economic activities on the basis that inequality itself can be not only a stimulus for people trying to secure a better education and job but also act as a source of motivation for entrepreneurs to invest more.	*Redistribution with extractive institutions hypothesis*: Growth causes widening inequality due to an exclusive economic structure *ex-ante*, where the top income groups received a substantial portion of income from wealth and equity compensation while the situation is intensified due to redistribution practices *ex-post* which were neither inclusive nor pro-poor.
Negative	*Constraint hypothesis*: A high level of inequality cannot provide sufficient educational opportunities to the low-income segment of society, thereby preventing opportunities for social mobility and undermining the efficient allocation of resources, while economic growth can be spurred by redistributing capital from rich to the credit-constrained poor.	*Redistribution with inclusive institutions hypothesis*: Growth provides the impetus for material well-being to mitigate the problem of inequality on the basis of inclusive growth processes *ex-ante* and/or effective retrospective policies such as fiscal transfers and safety nets for redistribution *ex-post*.

Causality	From environmental quality to inequality	From inequality to environmental quality
Positive	*Free riding behaviour hypothesis*: Free riding behaviour may dominate, particularly taking into account the public goods nature of the environmental problem. This can be the case for the global corrective actions against climate change where the temptation to free ride tends to be high among relatively poorer countries, given the fact that the poorest half of the world's population is estimated to be responsible for only 10 per cent of carbon emissions in total.	*Willingness to pay hypothesis*: Rich people's behaviour and personal choices are more environmentally friendly than those of the poor as the rich will be more concerned about the future as their life expectancy is longer than that of the poor, thereby being more willing to pay for environmental conservation programmes as a result.

An integrated framework 53

	From economic growth to environmental quality	From environmental quality to economic growth
Negative	*Environmental vulnerability hypothesis*: The poor group of a population is likely to be exposed to climatic and other hazards as well as various unexpected disasters and polluted areas, whereas the rich are capable of protecting themselves from them.	*Tendency to overexploit hypothesis*: The poor group tends to overexploit natural capital (often non-renewable resources), while the rich group also tends to prefer, often with greater political power, a policy that involves exploiting the environment in order to invest the returns abroad or benefits from economic activities at the expense of the environment.
Causality	*From economic growth to environmental quality*	*From environmental quality to economic growth*
Positive	*Pollution halo hypothesis*: Economic growth supported by foreign investors will have positive effects on the environmental quality in the host country because multinational investors are often likely to have cleaner technologies underpinned by the technology spillover effect.	*Green growth hypothesis*: A country can sustain its economic growth by doubling its efforts in the use of renewable energy and thus environmental protection policy can be a driving force to sustain an economy by creating synergies with the process of economic growth.
Negative	*Scale effect hypothesis*: The economic growth process could exert serious pressure on the environment, particularly carbon dioxide emissions, the effect transmitted through trade liberalisation force that likely increases economic activity, thus energy use. This free trade dynamic further influences the mix of a country's production reflected by a comparative advantage over others.	*Pollution haven hypothesis*: The use of carbon dioxide emissions would result in advancing the industrialisation process in a sense that an increase in carbon dioxide emissions derived from a lack of environmental regulation will attract inward FDI from foreign investors who want to avoid costly regulatory compliance.

Briefly describing the four competing schools of thought, I first present the *positive relationship* advocates,[4] who hold that income inequality provides incentives for more effort in order to gain more, which implies that inequality in a society is the outcome of the free choice of individuals, according to their appetite for risk, or that redistribution depends on the preferences of a society. They claim that as a result, inequality will encourage intense competition that will eventually stimulate economic growth. This school of thought further insists that inequality may also contribute to an engagement in a wide range of economic activities on the basis that inequality itself can be not only a stimulus for people trying to secure a better education and job but also act as a source of motivation for entrepreneurs to invest more. According to this line of reasoning, it is believed that a society as a whole may be better off with inequality than with equality.

A contrasting school of thought,[5] on the other hand, argued that the negative impact of inequality on economic growth activities inevitably predominates. This school's view is that inequality cannot provide sufficient educational opportunities to the low-income segment of society, thereby preventing opportunities for social mobility and eventually hindering the development of human capital. In a more comprehensive manner, Wilkinson and Pickett (2010) investigated social problems in 23 countries with different levels of economic inequality, and found that the more unequal the country was, the worse it performed in various dimensions of society, which substantially hinders economic activities. Meanwhile, Berg and Ostry (2013) also identified some negative consequences of income inequality by exploring the differences in the sustainability of economic growth between Asia and Latin America. They attributed such consequences to the difficulty in investing in education for the poor, which would likely result in a middle-income trap. In his book, *The Great Escape*, Angus Deaton (2013), who was awarded the 2015 Nobel Prize for Economics, also popularised the notion of the negative impact of inequality on growth. He acknowledged that inequality may be both a by-product of growth and an incentive for growth but stressed that high levels of inequality could stifle growth when inequality derives from rent-seeking. In addition, high levels of inequality could undermine the efficient allocation of resources, aggravate corruption and promote favouritism, as the rich protect their vested interests.

In particular, greater attention should be paid to the study conducted by Bourguignon (2004). In it, he supported the negative relationship hypothesis with a focus on political economy channels. The first channel was explained by the role of the credit market redistributing capital from the rich to the credit-constrained poor and contributing to increased efficiency and investment, ultimately spurring economic growth. Embracing the median-voter principle, he also claimed that the more unequal societies are, the greater redistribution will be, then such redistribution through taxation distortedly disincentivises to save and invest, thereby retarding the pace of growth. He further expanded his discussion of the inequality–growth nexus into the triangle interaction by incorporating a poverty dimension into it. His policy emphasis mainly focuses on the goal of reducing poverty in the setting of national specific characteristics on the growth-enhancing, inequality-reducing distribution policies and their causalities mentioned earlier.

Meanwhile, a large body of literature in the sphere of the reverse causal relationship running from economic growth to inequality[6] supports the negative impact by providing empirical evidence claiming, in essence, that growth provides the impetus for material well-being to mitigate the problem of inequality on the basis of the two conditions: (1) sharing opportunities that generate higher job-creating potential in the inclusive growth process *ex-ante*; and (2) effective retrospective policies such as fiscal transfers and safety nets for redistribution *ex-post*. Such a desirable phenomenon has been frequently cited by policy advisors, who subscribe to the trickle-down effect (e.g. Basu and Mallick, 2008; Akinci, 2017). Especially, policymakers who design *ex-post* redistribution mechanisms should take into account the three classes of income distributions for their fiscal policy mix, which are (a) primary income distribution before tax and subsidies, (b) secondary income distribution after deduction of taxes and inclusion of transfer payments, and finally, (c) tertiary income distribution after taking imputed benefits from public expenditures. If not, unequalising force in the growth process could predominate in a society, which leads to a discussion on the final hypothesis.

The literature investigating a positive causality from economic growth to inequality has also received a fair amount of attention.[7] Rubin and Segal (2015), for instance, observed an upward trend in inequality in the United States during the post-war period (1953–2008) and attributed its rampant inequality to an exclusive economic structure *ex-ante*, where the top income groups received a substantial portion of income from wealth and equity compensation, both of which are sensitive to economic growth. These authors further claimed that the situation arose due to redistribution practices *ex-post* that were neither inclusive nor pro-poor. Additionally, in his influential book, Branko Milanovic (2016)[8] argued that the recent phenomenon of widening inequality in wealthy countries, especially in the United States and the United Kingdom, can be attributed to radical technological advances and labour mobility, underpinned by the effects of globalisation. Moreover, he conceptualised such rising inequality as an N-shaped relationship between national income per person and inequality, which is also regarded as a "second Kuznets curve" or "Kuznets waves."

In conclusion, these four different theoretical foundations may have caused contrasting or sometimes contradicting assertions, which is why no consensus has yet emerged for the economic growth–inequality nexus within a country (see Box 3.1).

BOX 3.1   INEQUALITY AND ECONOMIC GROWTH INTERACTIONS BY GROUPS OF COUNTRIES

Full analysis of the relationship between sustainable development and structural transformation entails addressing the bi-directional causation between the three components of sustainable development. An intermediate step towards this is to revisit the issue of economic inequality and growth interactions. This component of the research illustrates the complexity of the larger project of the relationship between all three dimensions of sustainable development and structural transformation.

The question of how to achieve inclusive structural transformation sits at the forefront of the current public policy agenda. For example, it was the main theme of the 2017 UN high-level political forum on sustainable development, "Eradicating Poverty and Promoting Prosperity in a Changing World" and of the 2017 "Africa Regional Forum on Sustainable Development, Ensuring Inclusive and Sustainable Growth and Prosperity for All." Discussions in these political fora were largely based on individual country experiences, including, the recent phenomenon of widening inequality in the United States and the United Kingdom (Milanovic, 2016). A substantial number of developing countries have also suffered from widening inequality despite a decade of strong growth.

According to the Gini coefficient over the period 2000–2009, on average, Latin America and Africa registered 0.522 and 0.439, while Asia, North America and Europe recorded 0.375, 0.367 and 0.325, respectively (AfDB, 2012). In 2010, six out of the ten most unequal countries worldwide were in Africa (Armah et al., 2014). Such high levels of inequality have been proven to be less poverty-reducing as the benefits of growth accrue to fewer individuals, hence the slower-than-anticipated pace of poverty reduction in the region. This seriously raised doubts about the sustainability of the development trajectories in many developing countries.

In this context, it is useful to see a preliminary analysis of the data, conducted by Baek (2018) in order to observe some empirical regularities. Figure 3.2 demonstrates some empirical regularities – the

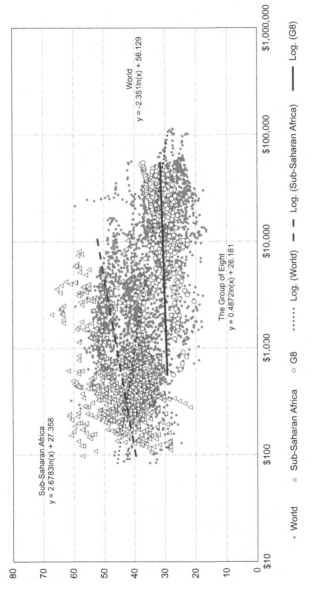

Figure 3.2 Inequality–growth dynamics: global, the Group of Eight (G8) and Sub-Saharan Africa. Source: Baek (2018).

negative association between inequality and growth in the group of 175 countries. Meanwhile, the coefficient of the logarithmic equation for this group is approximately −2.35. Further analysis by country group shows additional regularities – 18 Sub-Saharan African countries, widely considered the poorest group, appear to have a positive association with the logarithmic coefficient of 2.68, which can be inferred that higher growth is realised as income inequality increases and/or vice versa. Similarly, the Group of Eight (G8), the world's most highly industrialised economies, including Canada, France, Germany, Italy, Japan, Russia, the United Kingdom and the United States, is characterised by the positive relationship with the logarithmic coefficient of .49 although the magnitude of this coefficient is smaller than that of the poorest group.

In short, these empirical regularities provide meaningful implications that the world as a whole is approaching an environment where the more equal the income (re)distribution is, the greater economic growth is to be realised or vice versa, whereas both the poorest and the richest groups of countries are likely to suffer from the undesirable circumstances with which societies become more unequal or unfair as their economies grow. Hypothetically speaking based on the observed regularities, it can be said that there is a trend behind a country's developmental process under the *inequality–growth* nexus: as the process of growth begins from very low levels of income, inequality is likely to increase; after reaching a certain developmental stage, a country may transform into a society where its growth is translated into benefits for the poor; once shared broadly across society, an additional economic benefit has the tendency to be concentrated within the rich, which could aggravate an unequal income (re)distribution practice.

3.2.2 Inequality versus environmental quality

The complicated analysis could also apply to the second nexus in country change processes, which pertains to the relationship between inequality and environmental quality. The importance of this relation has stimulated a large amount of empirical research, but their empirical evidence is somewhat dissimilar. Drabo (2011) surveyed 31 econometric-driven studies on this nexus and concluded by summarising that ten studies supported a positive impact of inequality on environmental quality and the opposite direction (negative) was found in a further nine, while in 12 studies, causality running from inequality and environmental quality was not statistically significant.[9] On the one hand, the *negative relationship* advocates,[10] pioneered by James K. Boyce (1994), contended that widened inequality increases environmental degradation[11] because the poor group tends to overexploit natural capital (often non-renewable resources). Meanwhile, the rich group also tends to prefer a policy that involves exploiting the environment in order to invest the returns abroad. Boyce (2007) also sought to integrate political inequality into this hypothesis, arguing that rich people are more likely to have political power (in the form of making decisions) over the poor, thus tending to gain disproportionate benefits from economic activities at the expense of the environment, and hence, being in favour of environmentally damaging projects. This hypothesis in terms of unequal power dynamics has further been supported by the median-voter principle that the greater the inequality the less environmental R&D spending is likely to be (Magnani, 2000) and that a smaller pollution tax collection is expected to be set by the majority-elected representatives (Marsiliani and Renstrom, 2000). Boyce et al. (1999) examined the interactions between power distribution and the environment, with a particular use of data on voter participation and found a positive relationship, that is, greater power inequality is associated with greater environmental degradation.

With the aim of linking this nexus to health, Drabo (2011) investigated how environmental quality can be considered a mechanism through which inequality affects health. The findings showed that there is a negative causality running from inequality to health, while such negative consequences can be mitigated by institutional effectiveness. Drabo's findings are somewhat consistent with more recent empirical research conducted by Markandya et al. (2018), whose modelling results showed that low carbon policy intervention can strongly be associated with health benefits for both rich and poor. Compared with other countries, the net benefits are larger for India and China.

There have been, on the other hand, strong opponents who believe that inequality can accommodate environmental protection measures.[12] This school of thought has particularly adopted the perspective that rich people's behaviour and personal choices (the way of consumption and the use of renewable energy) are more environmentally friendly than those of the poor. Under this assumption, this school contends that if rich people were to take a unit of income from the poor, the demand for environmental conservation will increase (Hökby and Söderqvist, 2003; Baumol and Oates, 2012). This line of reasoning is also consistent with the logic that the rich will be more concerned about the future as their life expectancy is longer than that of the poor, thereby being more willing to pay for environmental conservation programmes as a result thereof (Scruggs, 1998). In addition, the concept of the "marginal propensity to emit" was introduced by Ravallion, Heil and Jalan (2000), who insisted that the poorest would have a higher albeit marginal propensity to emit than the wealthiest because a low-emission good requiring high technology is likely to be expensive and thus, highly likely to be consumed by the rich group rather than the poor.

Reverse causality also exists in the sense that an environmental crisis (or environmentally unsustainable growth) in itself increases inequality. Arguably, the poor group of a population is likely to be exposed to climatic and other hazards as well as various unexpected disasters and polluted areas.[13] That is, the poor are vulnerable to environmental risks, whereas the rich are capable of protecting themselves from them. Admitting this reasoning would further imply some vicious circle of environmental vulnerability that could have a significant impact on the social exclusion or social marginalisation of the poor. In fact, the relationships between the environment and poverty have been one of the most attractive research topics since the adoption of the 2030 Agenda and the Paris Agreement in 2015, both of which particularly prioritise the impact analysis from climate change on social development dynamics. Narloch and Bangalore (2018) studied its multifaceted relationship using the combination of geospatial data and a household survey in Vietnam and their empirical results clearly showed that poorer households are confronting greater environmental risks, although to varying degrees between rural and urban areas. This is fairly consistent with the study conducted by Scott (2006), who further brought the dimension of children into the table. Her main argument was that the concept of the environment should be defined as beyond a bio-physical setting in the sense that people are associated with each other and their surroundings. In this context, the chronically poor group who tend to be highly reliant on access to natural resources for their lives are most exposed to environmental changes where most of whom likely pass on their environmental vulnerability to their children.

However, this negative relationship running from the environmental quality to inequality (the resilience capability hypothesis) is not always the case when applying the logic of the tendency to overexploit hypothesis, albeit in a reverse direction, into it. Such tendency regardless of the poor or the rich may be intensified especially when more available natural resources are in place to be converted into capital. Relative to the poor group, the rich could be able to do conversion activities (from the environment to capital) massively by the superior capability of seeking economies of scale in exploitation or extraction. Free riding behaviour may dominate in this circumstance, particularly taking into account the public goods nature of the environmental problem.[14] The line of reasoning could be expanded further to the global corrective actions against climate change where the temptation to free ride tends to be high among relatively poorer countries (Aggarwal and Dupont, 2005), given the fact that the poorest half of the world's population is estimated to be responsible for only 10 per cent of carbon emissions in total, according to an Oxfam report (Gore, 2015).

3.2.3 Environmental quality versus economic growth

Like the earlier two, the third nexus in country change processes could also be explored under four conflicting hypotheses.[15] First, there is the *scale effect hypothesis*, under which it is contended that the economic growth process could exert serious pressure on the environment, particularly carbon dioxide emissions.[16] In this school of thought, this effect can most be transmitted through trade liberalisation force that likely increases economic activity, thus energy use. This free trade dynamic further influences the mix of a country's production reflected by a comparative advantage over others, which in turn reshapes a country's energy mix. Considering this hypothesis, Kivyiro and Arminen (2014) and many other scholars (e.g. Lotfalipour, Falahi and Ashena, 2010; Hamit-Haggar, 2012; Ozturk and Acaravci, 2013; Hwang and Yoo, 2014) have investigated the causal links between carbon dioxide emissions and economic development, widely employing the Granger causality-based error correction model approach. The majority of these studies have provided empirical support of statistically significant positive causality running from economic growth to carbon dioxide emissions (in other words, negative impact of economic growth on environmental quality), while also recognising that causality relationships vary greatly between countries.

There have been, on the other hand, studies claiming a reverse causality running from environmental pollution to economic growth, such that the use of carbon dioxide emissions would result in advancing the industrialisation process, which has been termed the *pollution haven hypothesis*.[17] The hypothesis is based on the economic logic that an increase in carbon dioxide emissions derived from a lack of environmental regulation will attract inward FDI from foreign investors who want to avoid costly regulatory compliance. For instance, Al-mulali et al. (2013) studied the long-run relationship between growth and carbon emissions in Latin American and Caribbean countries, where they found 60 per cent of the tested countries had a positive bi-directional long-run association while recognising that the other 40 per cent delivered mixed results. Similarly, Xue et al. (2014) examined the relationship between carbon dioxide emissions and the economic growth of nine European countries based on the Granger causality test and risk analysis on the impacts of the reduction of carbon dioxide emissions on growth. They found strong negative causality from the level of emissions to growth performance in all the tested countries and perhaps more importantly, their results indicated that the impact of emission reduction on growth varies by country, which further confirms that the sign and direction of causality depend on each country's experience in terms of growth and the sectoral composition of growth. Regarding which, the greatest negative impact is observed in Italy, followed by Portugal, while the lowest impact is estimated in Sweden as well as the United Kingdom.

Meanwhile, the *win–win* advocates have put forward strong enough evidence to make an important contribution to the environmental development discourse. Within this school of thought, there are two hypotheses: the *green growth hypothesis* and the *pollution halo hypothesis*.

The former is associated with the green economy, whereby a country could sustain its growth by doubling its efforts in the use of renewable energy and thus environmental protection policy can be a driving force to sustain an economy by creating synergies with the process of economic growth. The United Nations Environment Programme (UNEP) is notably leading such *Green Economy Initiatives* to inform the optimal pathway towards environmentally sustainable development (UNEP, 2011) with the introduction of an environment mainstreaming toolkit, namely the Integrated Green Economy Modelling Framework (IGEMF) (PAGE, 2017), followed by the Policy Coherence for Sustainable Development (PCSD) introduced from the OECD (2019), among others. In an empirical front, Lim, Lim and Yoo (2014) examined the short- and long-run causality between carbon emissions and economic growth in the Philippines for the period 1965–2012 and concluded that economic growth continues without an increase in carbon emissions, based on identified uni-directional causality running from emissions to growth. Moreover, Sebri and Ben-Salha (2014) investigated the causal orientation between growth and renewable energy in the BRICS countries over the period 1971–2010. Their empirical results imply a bi-directional Granger causality between the two and the important role of renewable energy in sustaining growth.

Under the latter perspective,[18] it is pointed out that economic growth supported by foreign investors will have positive effects on the environmental quality in the host country because multinational investors are often likely to have cleaner technologies, which can be referred to as the *halo effect*. The school of thought further claims that foreign firms would transfer the renewable technologies to local ones, underpinned by technology spillover effects. This has been the case especially for developing countries to which green technologies from advanced nations were transferred (Golub, Kauffmann and Yeres, 2011), while Eskeland and Harrison (2003) empirically supported this hypothesis that investment by the United States to several developing countries was mostly accompanied by energy-efficient and clean technologies. In a broader sense, Pao and Tsai (2011) applied the cointegration and causality tests for this relationship in Russia and found that, in the long run, emissions appear to be output inelastic, such that output tends to have a negative impact on emissions. Particularly, the most recent empirical study on this theme is worthy of our critical review, which was conducted by Ike, Usman and Sarkodie (2020). Employing the Method of Moments Quantile Regression with fixed effects, they investigated the effect of oil production dynamics on carbon emissions over the period 1980–2010. What they found was that increased oil production is associated with greater levels of carbon emissions with strong effects at the lowest quantile while only marginal effects at the highest quantile. More interestingly, the electricity production level appears to increase the emission level while trade likely condenses greenhouse emissions across all the quantiles. This final point firmly validates the pollution halo hypothesis for oil-producing countries.

3.3 Interactions between country change processes and normative frameworks

What is the goal of the analysis of the trinity nexus? First, in the theoretical domain, the second Kuznets curve or the N-shaped relationship between national income per person and inequality, which is also regarded as a "second Kuznets curve" or "Kuznets waves" could be further explored based on embracing the four competing schools of thought. Similarly, the EKC could also be explained by the application of the *pollution haven hypothesis* and/or *scale effect hypothesis* for the first half of the conceptual time period and of the *green growth hypothesis* and/or *pollution halo hypothesis* for the second half. In particular, country change processes of the environment versus inequality have received relatively less theoretical attention in past literature. In this regard, my hypotheses of the *tendency to overexploit* and *resilience capability* as well as the *willingness to pay* and *free riding behaviour* could be used as a basis for extended Kuznets curves. In other words, the Kuznets curve hypothesis (of both the growth–inequality and the growth–environment interactions) could be augmented by incorporating the theoretical reviews undertaken in this chapter, while a new hypothetical curve on the basis of the environment–inequality nexus could be advanced, which are both visualised in Figure 3.3.

Another big policy implication is that such analysis could shed light on potential tensions between the three dimensions of sustainable development and the need for policy consideration of such tensions by national institutions and actors. Hence, this interaction analysis could provide very useful information when mainstreaming into the national development framework the global view of the 2030 Agenda that has located economic, social and environmental sustainability at the heart of the development process. For instance, the existing institutional planning architecture that was designed

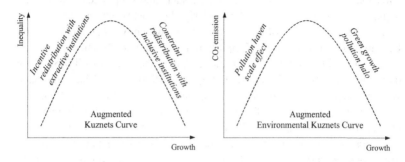

Figure 3.3 Augmented Kuznets curve hypotheses.

in accordance with the traditionally prioritised national strategy – *grow first and clean up later* – would be revised with an improved national framework that would allow countries not only to achieve accelerated growth but also ensure that such growth is inclusive and avoids or minimises environmental degradation (UN, 2021a).

Understanding the trinity nexus in country change processes can be a basis for exploring an untold story in the contemporary policy mix for sustainability transitions, which many developing countries are being confronted with, i.e. *Is it feasible simultaneously to achieve economic, social and environmental sustainability in the course of structural transformation?* and *How can there be a balance between trade-offs and synergies among economic, social and environmental aspects?* Unfolding such a story would allow us to assess further how country change processes can *filter out* from a normative framework to influence the formation of specific development strategies.

The question is then about "how to filter out." In a conceptual sense, country change processes influence national development strategies through individuals and institutions who could play an active role in deprioritising development areas that seem not to be salient to national development goals. The influential individuals, for instance, through government policies and collective action, create new change processes according to the creation of *ideas* for change. Hence, the *ideas* of major actors or individuals, followed by the formation of a reform discourse, play a mediating role in creating new institutional changes. Often, the formation of a new institution then weakens the legitimacy of the existing change processes and as a result, institutional change can take place.[19]

A mutual relationship between institutions and actors also plays a key determining role. That is, institutions and actors could be perceived to exist on the premise of working with each other (i.e. dualism), and not separately (Giddens, 1979). Under this perspective, institutions are therefore not separate from human actors. This is especially so in the transition period (of setting national development strategies) when the existing change processes are collapsing, and new ones are having to be created. It is also recognised that the ideas and actions of major actors are all very important within given constraints, namely the *path-dependence* feature (Campbell, 2004).

In short, country change processes drive adaptive change in national development strategies through institutions and actors. The change processes then contribute to the ongoing ones of designing an appropriate set of socioeconomic and environmental policies that are conducive to sustainable structural transformation. Yet, there is an additional layer that influences both Boxes 1 and 2 set out in the ISD framework. The next section is thus placed to explain how to fill this gap.

3.4 Exogenous drivers of change

I now move on to discussing some of the important exogenous drivers of change (Box 3) that significantly affect both normative framework and country change processes. While so many impacting drivers could be identified, I wish to, given the aforementioned scope of this study, centre upon (g) global debates on development strategies and (h) the global process of technological change. They are initially seen from a relatively global dimension, thus being exogenous to country change processes and to normative development frameworks and strategies. They are not, however, significantly affected by country change processes nor development frameworks and strategies of individual countries or governments of (small) low-income countries. Additionally, (i) initial socioeconomic conditions of a national context need to be considered as the third driver exogenously influencing country change processes and these are discussed before proceeding with the presentation of the four research chapters.

3.4.1 Global debates on development strategies

In response to the countervailing trends facing most developing countries (discussed in Chapter 1), a majority of them have attempted to identify new development thinking, that is, structural transformation as a development priority in their national development plans (Baek, 2019). In 2015, the adoption of the 2030 Agenda by the UN General Assembly refocused global attention on the centrality of structural transformation to be integrated into the Sustainable Development Goals (SDGs). The normative framework in this regard declares:

> strengthen the productive capacities of least developed countries in all sectors, including through *structural transformation* ... adopt policies which increase productive capacities, productivity and productive employment; financial inclusion; sustainable agriculture, pastoralist and fisheries development; sustainable industrial development; universal access to affordable, reliable, sustainable and modern energy services; sustainable transport systems; and quality and resilient infrastructure.
>
> (UN, 2015, para 27).

Greatly influenced by this global debate over development aspiration, a normative development framework is set and then adopted by national governments to inform country-specific development strategies. In essence, the normative framework could provide the range of strategic options open to individual country governments. Governments are then taken to have the freedom to choose between those informed by a normative vision that gives priority to structural transformation, and one that seeks to have a balance between economic growth (or prosperity), inequality reduction and environmental sustainability. Alternatively, governments decide to integrate the two, which would highly depend on their national contexts.[20]

Against this backdrop, the adoption of the 2030 Agenda and identification of a structural transformation agenda as a national priority clearly influences country change processes by reinforcing all the responsible and accountable governments and other actors to design more effective policymaking and institutions to promote their own development priority. Responding to the global force of sustainable development at the national level requires an integrated approach to the process of development that simultaneously addresses the multi-dimensions of sustainable development by various institutions and policy settings. This implies a need to break institutional silos, thus strengthening sectoral (*i.e.* horizontal) and sub-national (i.e. vertical) coordination within and among implementing entities.[21]

3.4.2 Global process of technological change

The second driver of change is associated with technological possibilities. This can be justified on the grounds that it facilitates structural transformation through its effect on productivity of the labour force, clean consumption and production processes for environmental conservation. Many empirical studies have found that structural transformation is largely driven by the adoption of capital-embodied technology (Caunedo, Jaume and

Keller, 2018) and that technology promotes inclusive development via the diffusion of information and knowledge[22] while minimising the potential negative effect of environmental degradation on human development. Other empirical studies, notably one conducted by Freeman (2015), have further provided evidence that technological change decreases the share of labour income, given that national income is split between the capital share of income and the labour share of income. As such, since capital is more unequally distributed, a higher capital share (i.e. investment in technology) means higher inequality. Moreover, robotisation and automation will further reduce labour's share, leading to more inequality (Baek, 2017; 2018).

However, there have been two competing views on whether technology should be considered exogenous or endogenous to country change processes. One of the most influential works that distinguished the technological effects from country change processes is that of Robert Solow (1956). His empirical results showed that per capita GDP in the United States doubled from the early 1900s to the 1950s and that the effect of capital on such growth was only 12.5 per cent, while the remaining 87.5 per cent was derived from technological change. That his study treated technology exogenously would lead to the conclusion that long-term equilibrium growth should also be determined outside the economic system. Such an exogeneity assumption was notably criticised by Arrow (1962)[23] and Romer (1990),[24] who introduced the endogenous growth model (with possibilities through the national dynamics of the labour force and the accumulation of knowledge, innovation and human capital) after having been involved in the competing discourses on a link of exogeneity versus endogeneity of technological change affecting country change processes.[25]

Reflecting on the set scope of this book, endogenising the technological effect can be difficult for low-income countries, compared with advanced nations. Hence, in this study, the focus is narrowed to the case where global debate on technological change is the source of some of the most profound exogenous shocks through the diffusion of innovation and technology transfer from outside a country's borders. It could thus reshape the policymaking orientation by being promptly adopted from outside in order to improve labour productivity, which would further restructure the national division of labour.

3.4.3 Initial socioeconomic conditions

With respect to the third exogenous driver of change, initial socioeconomic conditions are arguably so. Linking to the earlier discussion on the premise of institutions and their change processes, this driver is interpreted as a country heterogeneity largely shaped by the features of path dependency. For example, in the colonised nations of Africa and Latin America, where natural resources were abundant and climatic conditions were favourable for growing crops, but not for European settlement, the colonisers established extractive institutions to benefit their citizens back home (Acemoglu and Robinson, 2012). In particular, in Latin America, where a large number of slaves were deployed, conditions were ripe for establishing plantations, which generated extreme inequalities in terms of wealth, capital and political power (Engerman and Sokoloff, 2002). That is, these types of institutions were associated with limited economic growth and social exclusion, leading to significant levels of inequality in these regions. In contrast, in countries where the colonisers (i.e. mostly European settlers and their descendants) established institutions that promoted property rights for the majority, in the likes of Australia, Canada, New Zealand and the United States, some inclusiveness can be seen in their change processes. In this context, improving institutions that enable the right frameworks is essential for promoting inclusive sustainable development, where all stakeholders and actors deliver on shared responsibility to make sure that an effective policy coordination mechanism is in place; initial conditions do matter in this regard.

Notes

1 Grabel (2017) shed light on the lens of meso-level institutional governance as a raw material of change at the global and national levels. Her essential claim is that incoherence and discontinuity in global financial governance caused by the global crisis would have been productive rather than noise, as they provide more policy space for socioeconomic development of national institutions. Despite her *Hirschmanian* mindset (1958), for this study, a strong distinction between the global and national levels is drawn, which can thus downplay regional drivers of development strategy and ethnological change that may not be exogenous to country influences.

2 Various empirical studies found support for Kuznets's hypothesis (e.g. Papanek and Kyn, 1986; Chang and Ram, 2000), while more recent ones could not provide robust support for the hypothesis (e.g. Barro, 2000; Herzer and Vollmer, 2012). Especially, Barro somewhat agreed that the effect of income inequality is different contingent on the state of development. However, by using the panel data, the opposite of the inverted U-curve was found, in that inequality in poor nations (defined by per capita GDP below US\$2,070) stifles economic growth, while inequality in rich nations (defined by per capita GDP above US\$2,070) stimulates growth.

3 *Trickle-Down* refers to the policy stance that reduces taxes on businesses as a means to stimulate business investment, ultimately, in the longer term, benefitting society as a whole. On the other hand, *Trickle-Up* can be defined as the policy effect in which economic growth is best realised by lowering taxes on the (lower) middle classes who are likely to demand more goods and services (demand-led growth). Examples are: "broad-based personal income tax" intervention that is designed to impose the wealthier to pay a greater share of income in taxes than those less well off (Davis and Buffie, 2017); and "pro-poor indirect

tax" that is designed to increase taxation on transport while decreasing tax for food or energy in Mexico (Duclos, Makdissi and Araar, 2013).

4 For example, Friedman, 1953; Rebelo, 1991; Forbes, 2000; Bell and Freeman, 2001.

5 For example, Stiglitz, 1969; Bourguignon, 2004; Wilkinson and Pickett, 2010; Berg and Ostry, 2013; Lee and Son, 2016.

6 For example, de Janvry and Sadoulet, 2000; Adams, 2004; Basu and Mallick, 2008; Akinci, 2017.

7 For example, Cutler and Katz, 1991; Weriemmi and Ehrhart, 2008; Rubin and Segal, 2015; Milanovic, 2016.

8 Milanovic employed the scattergram analysis of a Gini of disposable per capita income and per capita GDP in the United States and the United Kingdom. The scattergram shows that in the United States the Gini index has increased constantly from 0.33 to 0.43 since the 1960s, as per capita GDP has grown, while in the United Kingdom the index has also gone up from 0.27 to 0.38 since 1978.

9 Despite the empirical complexities, some consensus on the negative relationship in the inequality–health status nexus has been reached (Mayer and Sarin, 2005) based on four theoretical principles: absolute income hypothesis (Khanam, Nghiem and Connelly, 2009); relative income hypothesis (Wilkinson, 1996); psychosocial hypothesis (Adamson, Ebrahim and Hunt, 2006); and the neo-materialism hypothesis (Lynch et al., 2000).

10 For example, Boyce, 1994; 2007; Torras and Boyce, 1998; Magnani, 2000; Marsiliani and Renstrom, 2000; Drabo, 2011; Laurent, 2014.

11 There have been various measures of environmental quality examined to support negative casualty. As a proxy indicator, biodiversity has been greatly used to explore a causal relation between economic inequality and biodiversity loss (e.g. measured by the portion of species threatened) (Holland, Peterson and Gonzalez, 2009).

12 For example, Scruggs, 1998; Ravallion, Heil and Jalan, 2000; Hökby and Söderqvist, 2003; Baumol and Oates, 2012.

13 For example, Scott, 2006; Stewart, 2014; Narloch and Bangalore, 2018.

14 For example, Aggarwal and Dupont, 2005; Carbone, 2007.

15 It should also be noted that there have been a number of empirical studies that find no significant relationship between economic growth and carbon dioxide emissions (e.g. Soytas, Sari and Ewing, 2007; Zhang and Cheng, 2009; Salahuddin, Gow and Ozturk, 2015).

16 For example, Jalil and Mahmud, 2009; Lotfalipour, Falahi and Ashena, 2010; Hamit-Haggar, 2012; Kohler, 2013; Ozturk and Acaravci, 2013; Hwang and Yoo, 2014; Kivyiro and Arminen, 2014.

17 For example, Dietzenbacher and Mukhopadhyay, 2007; Pao and Tsai, 2010; Al-mulali et al., 2013; Xue et al., 2014; Yang et al., 2018.

18 For example, Ozturk and Acaravci, 2010; Pao and Tsai, 2011; Arouri et al., 2012; Lim, Lim and Yoo, 2014.

19 For example, Campbell (2004), Anderson (2008), Béland (2009).

20 For example, socioeconomic and environmental conditions and development priorities as well as national institutions (largely influenced by the mechanism of path-dependence).

21 There are potential tensions between SDGs implementing institutions: economic growth strategies tend to be prioritised by the Ministries of Finance, of Economy and of Trade, while social inclusion is most likely pursued by the Ministries of

Labour and of Welfare, and environmental policies are primarily considered by the Ministries of the Environment, of Water and of Fisheries.

22   There is a growing awareness that the role of knowledge is critical for economic growth, especially in today's global marketplace. Driouchi, Azelmad and Anders (2006) conducted an empirical investigation into the effects of knowledge on economic performance using data of 1995–2001 for several groups of countries: Group of Seven and Europe; South and East Asia; Latin America; the Middle East and North Africa; and developing countries. The results from their modelling exercise are consistent with the prevalent viewpoint that knowledge is an essential driver of growth for all the groups tested. In particular, the results also explain the importance of the timing of investment in education and R&D as well as policy interventions for trade and FDI.

23   Arrow emphasised that, unlike products that cannot generally be used with other people (i.e. rivalry), knowledge does not compete with that of others (i.e. non-rival). However, the fact that knowledge is regarded as such does not mean that everyone can use it. Some knowledge can be excludable (i.e. excludability), depending on the legal and institutional apparatuses. Accordingly, most of the knowledge accumulated by R&D is highly likely to be excludable, thus tending to ensure high returns. Knowledge accumulation is also undertaken in everyday life through the *learning-by-doing* mechanism, and thus, technological advances based on these learning effects are caused by internal dynamic factors within the economy.

24   Romer demonstrated that there is a mechanism for achieving technological progress within the economy without an exogenous technological impact. He argued that endogenous technological progress can be achieved in an economy through investment in technology, knowledge accumulation and technology diffusion. Hence, under this theory, the role of R&D as an essential economic activity that can bring technological progress is emphasised. It is further asserted that in countries where the level of technology advancement is poor, technology adoption or spillover from the outside can also be a major driver for growth. However, it will be impossible for these countries to connect such technology to their economic growth without underlying human capital (UN, 2021b). Such capital needs to be accumulated so that existing knowledge can effectively be utilised. It can further create new knowledge and innovation based on existing knowledge, thereby enabling productivity improvement, which is a clear stimulus for growth.

25   Stokey (1998) emphasised the exogenous role of technical change for environmentally sustainable growth, while Aghion and Howitt (1998) claimed that exogenously imposed externalities cannot be the central reason for sustainable development. However, the assumption found in these two competing studies in that the elasticity of the marginal utility of consumption should be greater than one in order to attain a sustainable pace of growth in the models has been criticised by Lopez, Anriquez and Gulati (2007). Furthermore, there have been several empirical attempts to model sustainable development with a focus on the following: endogenous growth model in a two-sector small open economy (Eliasson and Turnovsky, 2004); learning-by-doing externalities under well-defined versus ill-defined property rights (McAusland, 2005); and optimal endogenous growth with exhaustible resources (Aseev and Kryazhimskii, 2007), among others.

References

Acemoglu, D. and Robinson, J., 2012. *Why nations fail: The origins of power, prosperity, and poverty*. New York: Crown Publishing Group.

Adams, R. Jr., 2004. Economic growth, inequality and poverty: Estimating the growth elasticity of poverty. *World Development*, 32(12), pp.1989–2014.

Adamson, J.A., Ebrahim, S. and Hunt, K., 2006. The psychosocial versus material hypothesis to explain observed inequality in disability among older adults: Data from the West of Scotland Twenty-07 Study, *Journal of Epidemiology and Community Health*, 60(11), pp.974–980.

AfDB (African Development Bank), 2012. *Income inequality in Africa*. Abidjan: AfDB (Briefing Note 5 for AfDB's Long-Term Strategy).

Aggarwal, V.K. and Dupont, C., 2005. Collaboration and coordination in the global political economy. In: J. Ravenhill, ed. *Global political economy*. 2nd ed. Oxford: Oxford University Press, pp.28–49.

Aghion, P. and Howitt, P., 1998. *Endogenous growth theory*. Cambridge, MA: MIT Press.

Akinci, M., 2017. Inequality and economic growth: Trickle-down effect revisited. *Development Policy Review*, 36(S1), pp.1–24

Al-mulali, U., Lee, Y.M.J., Mohammed, A.H. and Sheau-Ting, L., 2013. Examining the link between energy consumption, carbon dioxide emission, and economic growth in Latin America and the Caribbean. *Renewable and Sustainable Energy Reviews*, 26, pp.42–48.

Anderson, E., 2008. Experts, ideas, and policy change: The Russell Sage Foundation and small loan reform, 1909–1941. *Theory and Society*, 37(3), pp.271–310.

Armah, B., Keita, M., Gueye, A., Bosco, V., Ameso, J. and Chinzara, Z., 2014. Structural transformation for inclusive development in Africa: The role of active government policies. *Development*, 57(3–4), pp.438–451.

Arouri, M.H., Ben Youssef, A., M'henni, H. and Rault, C., 2012. Energy consumption, economic growth and CO2 emissions in Middle East and North African countries. *Energy Policy*, 45, pp.342–349.

Aseev, S.M. and Kryazhimskii, A.V., 2007. The Pontryagin maximum principle and optimal economic growth problems. *Proceedings of the Steklov Institute of Mathematics*, 257(1), pp.1–255.

Baek, S.J., 2017. Is rising income inequality far from inevitable during structural transformation? A proposal for an augmented inequality dynamics. *Journal of Economics and Political Economy*, 4(3), pp.224–237.

Baek, S.J., 2018. *The political economy of neo-modernisation: Rethinking the dynamics of technology, development and inequality*. London: Palgrave Macmillan.

Baek, S.J., 2019. Cooperating in Africa's sustainable structural transformation: Policymaking capacity and the role of emerging economies. *International Development Planning Review*, 41(4), pp.419–434.

Barro, R.J., 2000. Inequality and growth in a panel of countries. *Journal of Economic Growth*, 5(1), pp.5–32.

Basu, S. and Mallick, S., 2008. When does growth trickle-down to the poor? The Indian case. *Cambridge Journal of Economics*, 32(3), pp.461–477.

Baumol, W.J. and Oates, W.E., 2012. *The theory of environmental policy.* 2nd ed. Cambridge: Cambridge University Press.

Béland, D., 2009. Ideas, institutions, and policy change. *Journal of European Public Policy.* 16(5), pp.701–718.

Bell, L. and Freeman, R., 2001. The incentive for working hard: Explaining hours worked differences in the US and Germany. *Labour Economics*, 8(2), pp.181–202.

Berg, A.G. and Ostry, J.D., 2013. Inequality and unsustainable growth: Two sides of the same coin? *International Organisations Research Journal*, 8(4), pp.77–99.

Bourguignon, F., 2004. *The Poverty-growth-inequality triangle.* New Delhi: Indian Council for Research on International Economic Relations (wp125). Available from: http://siteresources.worldbank.org/INTPGI/Resources/342674 -1206111890151/15185_ICRIER_paper-final.pdf.

Boyce, J.K., 1994. Inequality as a cause of environmental degradation. *Ecological Economics*, 11(3), pp.169–178.

Boyce, J.K., 2007. *Is inequality bad for the environment?* Political Economy Research Institute-University of Massachusetts at Amherst (wp135). Available from: https://scholarworks.umass.edu/cgi/viewcontent.cgi?article=1108 &context=peri_workingpapers.

Boyce, J.K., Klemer, A.R., Templet, P.H. and Willis, C.E., 1999. Power distribution, the environment, and public health: A state-level analysis. *Ecological Economics*, 29, pp.127–140.

Campbell, J.L., 2004. *Institutional change and globalization.* Princeton, NJ: Princeton University Press.

Carbone, M., 2007. Supporting or resisting global public goods. *Global Governance*, 13(2), pp.179–198.

Caunedo, J., Jaume, D. and Keller, E., 2018. Structural transformation: Feedbacks from capital embodied technology adoption and capital-skill complementarity. In: Proceedings of the 2018 annual meeting of the society for economic dynamics, 28–30 June 2018, Mexico City. Mexico: Society for Economic Dynamics. Available from: https://editorialexpress.com/cgi-bin/conference/download.cgi ?db_name=SED2018&paper_id=1188.

Chang, J.Y. and Ram, R., 2000. Level of development, rate of economic growth, and income inequality. *Economic Development and Cultural Change*, 48(4), pp.787–799.

Cutler, D.M. and Katz, L.F., 1991. Macroeconomic performance and the disadvantaged. *Brookings Papers on Economic Activity*, 2, pp.1–61.

Davis, C. and Buffie, N., 2017. *Trickle-down dries up: States without personal income taxes lag behind states with the highest top tax rates.* Institute on Taxation and Economic Policy. Available from: https://itep.org/wp-content/ uploads/trickledowndriesup_1017.pdf [Accessed 12 Feb 2020].

de Janvry, A. and Sadoulet, E., 2000. Growth, poverty, and inequality in Latin America: A causal analysis, 1970–94. *Review of Income and Wealth*, 46(3), pp.267–287.

Deaton, A., 2013. *The great escape: Health, wealth, and the origins of inequality.* Princeton, NJ: Princeton University Press.

Dietzenbacher, E. and Mukhopadhyay, K., 2007. An empirical examination of the pollution haven hypothesis for India: Towards a green Leontief paradox? *Environmental and Resource Economics*, 36(4), pp.427–449.

Drabo, A., 2011. Impact of income inequality on health: Does environment quality matter? *Environment and Planning A*, 43(1), pp.146–165.

Driouchi, A., Azelmad, E.M. and Anders, G.C., 2006. An econometric analysis of the role of knowledge in economic performance. *Journal of Technology Transfer*, 31(2), pp.241–255.

Duclos, J.Y., Makdissi, P. and Araar, A., 2013. Pro-poor indirect tax reforms, with an application to Mexico. *International Tax and Public Finance*, 21(1), pp.87–118.

Eliasson, L. and Turnovsky, S.J., 2004. Renewable resources in an endogenously growing economy: Balanced growth and transitional dynamics. *Journal of Environmental Economics and Management*, 48(3), pp.1018–1049.

Elkington, J., 2018. 25 years ago I coined the phrase "Triple Bottom Line." Here's why it's time to rethink it. *Harvard Business Review* [Online], Sustainability. Available from: https://hbr.org/2018/06/25-years-ago-i-coined-the-phrase -triple-bottom-line-heres-why-im-giving-up-on-it [Accessed 10 December 2018].

Engerman, S.L. and Sokoloff, K.L., 2002. Factor endowments, inequality, and paths of development among new world economies. *Economia*, 3(2), pp.41–102.

Eskeland, G.S. and Harrison, A.E., 2003. Moving to greener pastures? Multinationals and the pollution haven hypothesis, *Journal of Development Economics*, 70(1), pp.1–23.

Fischer, J., Gardner, T.A., Bennett, E.M., Balvanera, P., Biggs, R., Carpenter, S., Daw, T., Folke, C., Hill, R., Hughes, T.P., Luthe, T., Maass, M., Meacham, M., Norstrom, A.V., Peterson, G., Queiroz, C., Seppelt, R., Spierenburg, M. and Tenhunen, J., 2015. Advancing sustainability through mainstreaming a social-ecological systems perspective. *Current Opinion in Environmental Sustainability*, 14, pp.144–149.

Forbes, K., 2000. A reassessment of the relationship between inequality and growth. *American Economic Review*, 90(4), pp.869–897.

Freeman, R.B., 2015. Who owns the robots rules the world. *IZA World of Labor*, 5, pp.1–10.

Friedman, M., 1953. Choice, chance and the personal distribution of income. *Journal of Political Economy*, 61(4), pp.277–290.

Giddens, A., 1979. *Central problems in social theory: Action, structure, and contradiction in social analysis.* Berkeley, CA: University of California Press.

Golub, S.S., Kauffmann, C. and Yeres, P., 2011. *Defining and Measuring Green FDI: An Exploratory Review of Existing Work and Evidence.* Paris: OECD (WP 2011/102).

Gore, T., 2015. *Extreme carbon inequality: Why the Paris climate deal must put the poorest, lowest emitting and most vulnerable people first.* Oxford: Oxfam International.

Grabel, I., 2017. *When things don't fall apart: Global financial governance and developmental finance in an age of productive incoherence.* Cambridge, MA: MIT Press.

Hamit-Haggar, M., 2012. Greenhouse gas emissions, energy consumption and economic growth: A panel cointegration analysis from Canadian industrial sector perspective. *Energy Economics*, 34(1), pp.358–364.

Haughton, G. and Counsell, D., 2004. Regions and sustainable development: Regional planning matters. *Geographical Journal*, 70(2), pp.135–145.

Herzer, D. and Vollmer, S., 2012. Inequality and growth: Evidence from panel cointegration. *Journal of Economic Inequality*, 10(4), pp.489–503.

Hirschman, A.O., 1958. *The strategy of economic development.* New Haven, CT: Yale University Press.

Hökby, S. and Söderqvist, T., 2003. Elasticities of demand and willingness to pay for environmental services in Sweden. *Environmental and Resource Economics*, 26(3), pp.361–383.

Holland, T.G., Peterson, G.D. and Gonzalez, A., 2009. A cross-national analysis of how economic inequality predicts biodiversity loss. *Conservation Biology*, 23(5), pp.1304–1313.

Hwang, J.H. and Yoo, S.H., 2014. Energy consumption, CO2 emissions, and economic growth: Evidence from Indonesia. *Quality & Quantity*, 48(1), pp.63–73.

Ike, G.N., Usman, O. and Sarkodie, S.A., 2020. Testing the role of oil production in the environmental Kuznets curve of oil producing countries: New insights from method of moments quantile regression, *Science of The Total Environment*, 711, pp.135208.

Jalil, A. and Mahmud, S.F., 2009. Environment Kuznets curve for CO2 emissions: A cointegration analysis for China. *Energy Policy*, 37(12), pp.5167–5172.

Khanam, R., Nghiem, H.S. and Connelly, L.B., 2009. Child health and the income gradient: Evidence from Australia. *Journal of Health Economics*, 28(4), pp.805–817.

Kivyiro, P. and Arminen, H., 2014. Carbon dioxide emissions, energy consumption, economic growth, and foreign direct investment: Causality analysis for sub-Saharan Africa. *Energy*, 74, pp.595–606.

Kohler, M., 2013. CO2 emissions, energy consumption, income and foreign trade: A South African perspective. *Energy Policy*, 63, pp.1042–1050.

Kuznets, S., 1955. Economic growth and income inequality. *American Economic Review*, 45(1), pp.1–28.

Laurent, É., 2014. *Inequality as pollution, pollution as inequality: The social-ecological nexus.* The Stanford Center on Poverty and Inequality. Available from: https://inequality.stanford.edu/sites/default/files/media/_media/working_papers/laurent_inequality-pollution.pdf.

Lee, D.J. and Son, J.C., 2016. Economic growth and income inequality: Evidence from dynamic panel investigation. *Global Economic Review*, 45(4), pp.331–358.

Lim, K.M., Lim, S.Y. and Yoo, S.H., 2014. Oil consumption, CO2 emission, and economic growth: Evidence from the Philippines. *Sustainability*, 6(2), pp.967–979.

Lopez, R.E., Anriquez, G. and Gulati, S., 2007. Structural change and sustainable development. *Journal of Environmental Economics and Management*, 53(3), pp.307–322.

Lotfalipour, M.R., Falahi, M.A. and Ashena, M., 2010. Economic growth, CO2 emissions, and fossil fuels consumption in Iran. *Energy*, 35(12), pp.5115–5120.

Lynch, J.W, Smith, G.D., Kaplan, G.A. and House, J.S., 2000. Income inequality and mortality: Importance to health of individual income, psychosocial environment, or material conditions. *British Medical Journal*, 320(7243), pp.1200–1204.

Magnani, E., 2000. The environmental Kuznets curve, environmental protection policy and income distribution. *Ecological Economics*, 32(3), pp.431–443.

Markandya, A., Sampedro, J., Smith, S.J., Van Dingenen, R., Pizarro-Irizar, C., Arto, I. and González-Eguino, M., 2018. Health co-benefits from air pollution and mitigation costs of the Paris agreement: A modelling study. *The Lancet Planetary Health*, 2, pp.e126–133.

Marsiliani, L. and Renstrom, T.I., 2000, *Inequality, environmental protection and growth*. Tilburg University (CentER Discussion Paper; Vol. 2000-34). Available from: https://pure.uvt.nl/ws/portalfiles/portal/535444/34.pdf.

Mayer, S.E. and Sarin, A., 2005. Some mechanisms linking economic inequality and infant mortality. *Social Science & Medicine*, 60(3), pp.439–455.

McAusland, C., 2005. Learning by doing in the presence of an open access renewable resource: Is growth sustainable? *Natural Resource Modeling*, 18(1), pp.41–68.

Milanovic, B., 2016. *Global inequality: A new approach for the age of globalization*. Cambridge: Harvard University Press.

Narloch, U. and Bangalore, M., 2018. The multifaceted relationship between environmental risks and poverty: New insights from Vietnam. *Environment and Development Economics*, 23(3), pp.298–327.

Nissanke, M., 2019. Exploring macroeconomic frameworks conducive to structural transformation of sub-Saharan African economies. *Structural Change and Economic Dynamics*, 48, pp.103–116.

OECD (Organisation for Economic Co-operation and Development), 2019. *Recommendation of the Council on Policy Coherence for Sustainable Development* (OECD/LEGAL/0381). Paris: OECD.

Osman, R.H., Alexiou, C. and Tsaliki, P., 2012. The role of institutions in economic development: Evidence from 27 Sub-Saharan African countries. *International Journal of Social Economics*, 39(1/2), pp.142–160.

Ozturk, I. and Acaravci, A., 2010. CO2 emissions, energy consumption, and economic growth in Turkey. *Renewable and Sustainable Energy Reviews*, 14(9), pp.3220–3225.

Ozturk, I. and Acaravci, A., 2013. The long-run and causal analysis of energy, growth, openness and financial development on carbon emissions in Turkey. *Energy Economics*, 36, pp.262–267.

PAGE (Partnership for Action on Green Economy), 2017. *The integrated green economy modelling framework: Technical document*. Nairobi: UNEP.

Pao, H.T. and Tsai, C.M., 2010. CO2 emissions, energy consumption and economic growth in BRIC countries. *Energy Policy*, 38, pp.7850–7860.

Pao, H.T. and Tsai, C.M., 2011. Multivariate Granger causality between CO2 emissions, energy consumption, FDI (foreign direct investment) and GDP (gross domestic product): Evidence from a panel of BRIC (Brazil, Russian Federation, India, and China) countries, *Energy*, 36(1), pp.685–693.

Papanek, G. and Kyn, O., 1986. The effect on income distribution of development, the growth rate, and economic strategy. *Journal of Development Economics*, 23(1), pp.55–65.

Ravallion, M., Heil, M. and Jalan, J., 2000. Carbon emissions and income inequality. *Oxford Economic Papers*, 52(4), pp.651–669.

Rebelo, S., 1991. Long-run policy analysis and long-run growth. *Journal of Political Economy*, 99(3), pp.500–521.

Rubin, A. and Segal, D., 2015. The effects of economic growth on income inequality in the US. *Journal of Macroeconomics*, 45, pp.258–273.

Salahuddin, M., Gow, J. and Ozturk, I., 2015. Is the long-run relationship between economic growth, electricity consumption, carbon dioxide emissions and financial development in Gulf Cooperation Council Countries robust? *Renewable and Sustainable Energy Reviews*, 51, pp.317–326.

Scott, L., 2006. *Chronic poverty and the environment: A vulnerability perspective.* Overseas Development Institute (CPRC WP 62). Available from: https://www.odi.org/sites/odi.org.uk/files/odi-assets/publications-opinion-files/3429.pdf [Accessed 17 February 2020].

Scruggs, L.A., 1998. Political and economic inequality and the environment. *Ecological Economics*, 26(3), pp.259–275.

Sebri, M. and Ben-Salha, O., 2014. On the causal dynamics between economic growth, renewable energy consumption, CO2 emissions and trade openness: Fresh evidence from BRICS countries. *Renewable and Sustainable Energy Reviews*, 39, pp.14–23.

Solow, R.M., 1956. A contribution to the theory of economic growth. *Quarterly Journal of Economics*, 70(1), pp.65–94.

Soytas, U., Sari, R. and Ewing, B.T., 2007. Energy consumption, income, and carbon emissions in the United States. *Ecological Economics*, 62(3), pp.482–489.

Stewart, F., 2014. Sustainability and inequality. *Development*, 57(3–4), pp.344–361.

Stiglitz, J.E., 1969. Distribution of income and wealth among individuals. *Econometrica*, 37(3), pp.382–397.

Stokey, N.L., 1998. Are there limits to growth? *International Economic Review*, 39(1), pp.1–31.

Torras, M. and Boyce, J.K., 1998. Income, inequality, and pollution: A reassessment of the Environmental Kuznets Curve. *Ecological Economics*, 25, pp.147–160.

UN (United Nations), 2015. *Transforming our world: The 2030 agenda for sustainable development.* New York: UN.

UN, 2021a. *Exploring climate action in Kuwait: A focus on environmentally sustainable finance.* Kuwait: UN. Available from: https://kuwait.un.org/en/download/76508/142240 [Accessed 10 September 2021].

UN, 2021b. *Unlocking human capital potential in Kuwait as global actor in the knowledge economy.* Kuwait: UN. Available from: https://kuwait.un.org/en/download/76503/134060 [Accessed 10 September 2021].

UNEP (United Nations Environment Programme), 2011, *Towards a green economy: Pathways to sustainable development and poverty eradication: A synthesis for policy makers.* Nairobi: UNEP.

UNEP, 2015. *Building inclusive green economies in Africa: Experience and lessons learned 2010–2015.* Nairobi: UNEP.

Weriemmi, M. and Ehrhart, C., 2008. Inequality and growth in a context of commercial openness, theoretical analysis and empirical study: The case of the countries around the Mediterranean Basin. *Journal of Social Management*, 6(2), pp.81–91.

Wilkinson, R., 1996. *Unhealthy societies: The afflictions of inequality.* London: Routledge.

Wilkinson, R. and Pickett, K., 2010. *The spirit level: Why equality is better for everyone.* London: Penguin.

Xue, B., Geng, Y., Müller, K., Lu, C. and Ren, W., 2014. Understanding the causality between carbon dioxide emission, fossil energy consumption and economic growth in developed countries: An empirical study. *Sustainability*, 6(2), pp.1037–1045.

Yang, J., Guo, H., Liu, B., Shi, R., Zhang, B. and Ye, W., 2018. Environmental regulation and the pollution haven hypothesis: Do environmental regulation measures matter? *Journal of Cleaner Production*, 202, pp.993–1000.

Zhang, X. and Cheng, X., 2009. Energy consumption, carbon emissions, and economic growth in China. *Ecological Economics*, 68(10), pp.2706–2712.

4 Prioritising interventions for sustainable structural transformation

A structural equation modelling approach

4.1 Introduction

In 2015, the adoption of the 2030 Agenda for Sustainable Development called on signatory countries to ensure that their development outcomes were socially, economically and environmentally sustainable. Furthermore, the Sustainable Development Goals (SDGs) that it set out were and are integrated and multi-sectoral implying that interventions in one sector can have catalytic impacts on other sectors and could thereby accelerate the achievement of the development goals. For developing countries, particularly in Africa, the SDGs are viewed as a means of structurally transforming their largely agrarian and commodity-dependent countries into manufacturing hubs. Indeed, in recent years, Africa has made industrialisation a major policy priority in the context of its continental development framework and policy commitments (AUC, 2015).

However, given the large number of targets and indicators within the SDGs, policy prioritisation and sequencing are critical when it comes to resource optimisation and impact (Armah and Baek, 2018; Baek, 2019). In this context, it is important for policymakers to identify catalytic interventions to drive the transformation process. However, studies of the drivers of structural transformation have disproportionately analysed economic factors ahead of the other two main factors (social and environmental). Besides, few studies have examined the combined effect of social, economic and environmental determinants of structural transformation. This chapter thus seeks to determine the relative importance of economic, social and environmental interventions in catalysing structural transformation in Africa.

Since 2005, several African countries have made significant progress in sustaining positive growth, improving their performance on social indicators, such as health and education, and maintaining relatively low levels of greenhouse gas emissions. Real GDP volume increased in this continent by 54

DOI: 10.4324/9781003259916-4

per cent between 2004 and 2014, which is more than twice the global average rate of 24 per cent (UNCTAD, 2016). However, growth in most African countries has not been inclusive and trends in socioeconomic indicators have been mixed. For instance, primary enrolment has increased but drop-out rates are high and increasing at higher levels of education, perhaps suggesting that (secondary) education in these countries is still not of sufficient quality. Rates of maternal and child deaths have declined but remain the highest globally. Meanwhile, access to social services has been skewed in favour of high-income groups and urban dwellers. Indeed, according to the Gini coefficient, over the period 2000–2009, inequality in Africa (0.439) was second only to Latin America (0.522). The corresponding figures for Asia, North America and Europe were 0.375, 0.367 and 0.325, respectively. In 2010, six out of the ten most unequal countries worldwide were in Africa (Armah et al., 2014).

High dependence on primary commodity exports and limited value addition characterises much of Africa and has largely been associated with limited success in economic diversification. Unemployment (and underemployment) remains an enduring feature of the development landscape in Africa, particularly in Sub-Saharan Africa, where nearly 70 per cent of jobs are considered vulnerable, and youth and female labour force participation remain very low (ECA et al., 2016). Extreme poverty (defined as earning less than US$1.25 per day) in Sub-Saharan Africa, for instance, declined by a mere 14 per cent over the period 1990–2012. Meanwhile, 109 million more people were classified as extremely poor (people living in extreme poverty) during the same period (UNSD, 2016).

With respect to the environment, greenhouse gas emissions in Africa are very low by global standards but have been rising at a rapid rate since the 2010s. Meanwhile, adaption to climate change in Africa is weak and, importantly, the recent socioeconomic activities in Africa have not led to industrial development. Few African countries have succeeded in increasing the contribution of their industrial sector to their GDP. On the contrary, unlike developed countries, most African countries have transitioned from agriculture to the service sector.

It is against this backdrop that the 2030 Agenda for Sustainable Development has located economic, social and environmental sustainability at the heart of the development process. In this context, this development initiative urges both advanced and developing countries to integrate environmental, social and economic sustainability in their development planning frameworks and to avoid the untenable "grow first and clean up later" strategy pursued by the majority of the currently industrialised countries (UN, 2019). The obvious implication of this is that countries not only have to achieve accelerated growth but must also ensure that such growth is inclusive and avoids or minimises environmental degradation.

This raises important questions. First, is it feasible to simultaneously achieve economic, social and environmental sustainability? If not, in what order should these three types of sustainability be pursued? Moreover, would the successful implementation of such policies advance Africa's transformation agenda?

Few developed countries have been successful in simultaneously achieving rapid, green and inclusive growth. Indeed, the experiences of industrialised and emerging countries highlight potential trade-offs between economic growth, social inclusion and environmental conservation. For instance, China's transformation has been associated with rapid growth and steep declines in poverty, yet inequality and greenhouse gas emissions have increased markedly (Armah and Baek, 2015). How different would the transformation outcomes have been had China prioritised social inclusion or environmental conservation over growth in the initial stages of its development process? As the sustainable development paradigm discourages the policy option of growing first and cleaning up later, the need for strategic policy prioritisation and sequencing to leverage synergies, minimise trade-offs and optimise resource use is greater now than ever before.

The central objective of this chapter is therefore to identify the optimal sequence of social, economic and environmental conservation interventions that would minimise trade-offs and advance structural transformation in Africa. This objective is achieved by employing a structural equation model to estimate the direct and indirect impacts of social, economic and environmental indicators of sustainable development on a composite index of structural transformation. The contribution of this chapter is that it provides a framework for policymakers to prioritise and sequence policy interventions aimed at achieving structural transformation. It does so by quantifying the total (direct and indirect) impact of economic, social and environmental interventions on structural transformation.

In pursuit of this objective, the rest of the chapter is structured into five sections. I first review the literature on the social, economic and environmental drivers of structural transformation (Section 4.2). This is followed by a section on indicators (Section 4.3) and then a discussion of the methodology (Section 4.4). Section 4.5 then interprets the modelling results before the chapter concludes with a summary and policy implications in Section 4.6.

4.2 Literature review

Theoretical evidence on the socioeconomic and environmental drivers of structural change is scant compared with that of economic factors. The literature is also fragmented in the sense that there is no accepted theory on how the social, economic and environmental factors interact to influence structural transformation. Given the interlinkages existing between the social, economic and environmental factors that influence the transformation process, it is not enough to examine their impacts in isolation from each other. While some empirical studies have examined the synergies and trade-offs between the social, economic and environmental indicators of sustainable development, virtually none have linked their findings to structural transformation. For instance, in a recent study, Spaiser et al. (2017) conducted an empirical analysis of the underlying tensions and synergies between the social, economic and environmental dimensions of the SDGs using a structural equation model. To evaluate these interactions, the study categorised the SDGs into three latent constructs representing the economic (Goals 1, 2, 3, 6 and 11), social (Goals 4, 5, 8, 9, 10 and 16), and environmental (Goals 12, 13, 14 and 15) dimensions of sustainable development. The findings suggested that economic growth-focused strategies could promote socioeconomic development while hindering the achievement of environmental goals. These findings are however not linked to structural transformation.

One of the few studies that link the three dimensions (economic, social and environmental) to structural transformation was conducted by Armah and Baek (2015) using panel data for 29 African countries for the period 1995–2011. They found that an integrated approach to sustainable development that takes into account the economic, social and environmental dimensions has the most beneficial impact on Africa's structural transformation process.

In effect, with few exceptions, the collective impact of economic, social and environmental interventions on structural transformation has largely been overlooked in the literature. Adopting a holistic approach is nevertheless important since the synergies and potential trade-offs among the social, economic and environmental drivers can have a net positive or adverse impact on structural transformation (Baek, 2018). The conceptual framework of this study is presented in Figure 4.1. The rest of this section reviews the relevant literature on the economic, social and environmental drivers of structural transformation.

While there is broad consensus that structural transformation is associated with economic growth and development, there has been considerable debate about what drives transformation. Traditional notions of structural transformation emphasise sectoral shifts from agriculture to industry and services, underpinned by differences in inter-sectoral productivity. Timmer (2017) invoked a broader definition, capturing rural-urban migration. He defined structural transformation as being composed of the following features: a relative decline in the sectoral shares of low-productivity agriculture and low value-added extractive activities; a relative increase

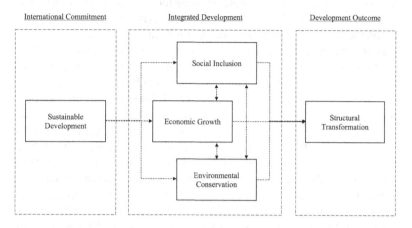

Figure 4.1 Conceptualising the relationship between sustainable development and structural transformation.

in manufacturing and high-productivity services; a decline in the relative share of agricultural employment in GDP; increasing rural-to-urban migration that stimulates the process of urbanisation; and the rise of a modern industrial and service economy.

4.2.1 Economic drivers of structural transformation

Overall, there is broad agreement among scholars that structural transformation is positively related to economic development but there is no scholarly consensus on the economic drivers of structural transformation, and there is considerable debate about the direction of causality (Herrendorf, Rogerson and Valentinyi, 2013).

On the one hand, structural transformation stimulates growth by reallocating resources from low- to high-productivity activities. In particular, the manufacturing sector is a source of growth and productivity because the sector embodies technology and innovation as well as entrepreneurial activity (Shen, Dunn and Shen, 2007, UNCTAD, 2018). The alternative view that growth causes transformation is based on the neoliberal premise that export-led development based on the principle of comparative advantage stimulates growth which, over time, causes structural transformation by accelerating the transition from an emphasis on agriculture to an emphasis on industry and services (Teignier, 2018). Rising income growth also influences structural transformation because preferences are non-homothetic; as incomes rise, households spend relatively less on agricultural goods and more on manufactured goods and services thereby promoting industrial sector development (Swiecki, 2017).

The empirical studies of the relationship between growth and structural transformation have, however, yielded mixed results. For instance, structural transformation in South Korea has been associated with the role of international trade in accelerating the transition from agriculture into industry and services (Sposi, 2019). Similarly, Ungor (2017) found that differences in sectoral productivity growth rates accounted for the different sectoral reallocations in Latin America and East Asia. However, other studies using Granger causality analysis have found that the causal relationship is country-specific, implying that there is no universal relationship between the two variables (Elliott, 1998). Furthermore, a cross-country analysis of 53 African countries found a U-shaped relationship between income growth and the manufacturing sector's contribution to GDP; below a threshold of US$943 (current value), an increase in per capita GDP is accompanied by a decrease in the manufacturing share of GDP, but beyond this level, incomes are positively associated with the manufacturing sector's contribution to GDP (Mijiyawa, 2017).

4.2.2 Social drivers of structural transformation

The relationship between growth and social development has also generated scholarly interest with a focus on inequality and human capital as potential drivers of structural transformation (Baek, 2017). Studies that have focused on the relationship between inequality and structural transformation have yet to agree on the direction of causality. Some scholars (e.g. Deutsch and Silber, 2004; Martorano, Park and Sanfilippo, 2017) focused on the impact of structural transformation on inequality, influenced by the work of Kuznets (1955). Meanwhile, others (e.g. Banerjee and Newman, 1993; Piketty, 1997) have emphasised the impact of inequality on growth, while a third school of thought (Deaton, 2013) maintains that the relationship is bi-directional.

Regarding the impact of structural transformation on inequality, Kuznets (1955) postulated an inverted U-shaped curve relationship arguing that, overall, inequality is likely to initially rise as industrial transformation takes hold. This process is driven by the transfer of labour from the low-wage, low-inequality agricultural sector to a relatively high-wage, high-inequality industrial sector. However, unlike developed countries, developing countries have experienced an agriculture to service-sector transition that should lead to different distributional outcomes between the two country groups.

The empirical findings on the relationship between social development and structural transformation suggest that the outcome depends on the nature of the transformation. For instance, Dastidar (2012) found that where structural change is characterised by a transition from agriculture to industry, inequality did not increase in developing countries. On the other hand, inequality was found to rise in developing countries experiencing an agriculture-service transformation. In the latter case, the increase in inequality is more pronounced when the initial levels of inequality are already higher than average.

The level of inequality influences the size and composition of aggregate demand and thereby influences the market for industrial production (Nurkse, 1953). In a similar vein, more recently, scholars have highlighted misallocation and underutilisation of resources as outcomes of inequality that further hinder economic growth (Restuccia and Rogerson, 2017).

But inequality can influence structural transformation and growth by undermining household investments in human capital development (Stiglitz, 1996). Specifically, inequality undermines the capacity of vulnerable groups to invest in the education of their children and adversely influences decisions about fertility as poor groups "invest" in childbirth with the hope of increasing the aggregate household income. However, high fertility rates actually curtail the ability to invest in quality education for their children (de la Croix and Doepke, 2003). In line with these findings, Basu and Guariglia (2008) found that, in addition to differences in agricultural productivity, differences in initial years of schooling can explain why some countries industrialise later than others.

Angus Deaton (2013) popularised the notion of the negative impact of inequality on structural transformation. He acknowledged that inequality may be both a by-product of growth and an incentive for growth but stressed that high levels of inequality could stifle growth when inequality derives from rent-seeking. Besides, high levels of inequality undermine the efficient allocation of resources, aggravate corruption and promote favouritism as the rich protect their vested interests.

4.2.3 Environmental drivers of structural transformation

Little is known about the environmental drivers of structural transformation as most of the literature has focused on the environmental impact of structural transformation as opposed to the effects of environmental policies on structural transformation. The Environmental Kuznets Curve provides theoretical insights into the environmental impacts of structural transformation. It postulates an inverted "U-curve" relationship between growth and environmental degradation (López-Menéndez, Pérez and Moreno, 2014). Others have rejected this argument by highlighting the role of technological innovation and advancements in renewable energies in decoupling degradation, particularly greenhouse gas emissions, from the growth process (Collier and Venables, 2012; Simon, 2013).

Causal evidence regarding the environmental drivers of structural transformation is limited. The empirical findings have so far supported the theoretical hypothesis of trade-offs between growth and environmental degradation but have highlighted the mediating role of policy in this relationship. One strand of research has centred on the role of the Green Revolution in influencing transformation through increases in agricultural productivity. In this context, Moscona (2018) found that agricultural productivity impeded structural transformation during the Green Revolution.

Other studies have focused on the relationship between the environment and development. For instance, Qizilbash (2010) found that countries that perform well in indicators of well-being and poverty had the highest levels of environmental degradation. He found Costa Rica to be an exception in this case and concluded that policies were vital to addressing the potential trade-offs between economic, social and environmental objectives. Beyond the productivity and welfare effects of environmental policies, environmental hazards, amplified by climate change, can have adverse impacts on productivity through their destructive impact on infrastructure. Furthermore, efforts to adapt to climate change could result in regulations that restrict industrial development.

4.3 Selection of indicators

To evaluate the collective contributions of the social, economic and environmental drivers of structural transformation, we identify proxy indicators for each of the drivers as well as structural transformation. We then construct a panel (balanced) data set comprising 29 African countries[1] for the period 1995–2011 using data from various sources, including the World Bank's World Development Indicators (WDI) database (2016), the IMF World Economic Outlook (WEO) database (2016) and the FAO Statistics Division database (2016).

The study employs commonly used sustainable development indicators on the basis of the SDGs. In this process, I avoid indicators that are transversal or transcend the economic, social and environmental drivers of structural transformation. However, it is important to note that the selection of indicators for each of the four groups of indicators is constrained by a lack of reliable data (Osman, Alexiou and Tsaliki, 2012). The rationale behind the proxy indicator selection is discussed below and then summarised in Table 4.1.

4.3.1 Economic growth indicators[2]

According to the majority of economic transformation literature, growth promotes structural transformation by altering sectoral productivity

Table 4.1 Classification and variable description

Dimension	Area of importance	Proxy indicator and description	Source
Economic development	Economic growth	Per capita GDP (annual %)	WDI
	Investment	Total investment (% of GDP)	WEO
	Green economy	Renewable energy consumption (% of total final energy consumption)	WDI
	Energy use	Energy intensity level of primary energy	WDI
Social inclusion	Poverty	Unemployment rate (% of the total labour force)	WDI
	Sanitation	Sanitation facilities (% of the population with access)	WDI
	Life quality	Life expectancy at birth (years)	WDI
	Maternal health	Adolescent fertility rate (births per 1,000 women ages 15-19)	WDI
Environmental conservation	Climate change	Emissions of carbon dioxide (metric tons per capita)	WDI
	Agriculture land	Arable land (hectares per person)	WDI
	Forests	Forest area (square km)	WDI
	Water	Improved water source (% of the population with access)	WDI
Structural transformation	Higher agricultural productivity by achieving a higher cereal yield	Cereal yield (kg per hectare) Agriculture gross per capita production index (2004 – 2006 = 100)	WDI FAOSTAT
	Higher share of manufacturing in value addition	Manufacturing value-added (% of GDP)	WDI
	Increases in the share of ICT in services exports	Services value-added (% of GDP)	WDI
	Better telecommunications infrastructure	Internet users (per 100 people)	WDI
	Improving health services by decreasing infant mortality rate	Infant mortality rate (per 1,000 live births)	WDI
	More developed financial market	Domestic credit provided by financial sector (% of GDP)	WDI

rates. Hence, taking into account data availability, the economic drivers of structural transformation comprise the following indicators of growth and productivity: per capita income growth (per capita GDP); investment (investment/GDP ratio); energy use (energy intensity level of primary energy); and green growth (renewable energy consumption as a share of total energy consumption).

GDP per capita measures the quantitative expansion of the economy and is indeed one of the most widely used measures of economic development, but it has been criticised as an inappropriate measure of well-being by some scholars (Giddings, Hopwood and O'Brien, 2002).[3] Investments can fuel growth by increasing capital stock and also improving factor productivity. Investments in infrastructure in particular can unlock binding constraints to development and enhance total factor productivity. Energy efficiency and intensity determine productivity and growth (Vera and Langlois, 2007). The energy supply to GDP ratio is thus used to capture energy efficiency; lower ratios imply greater efficiencies in the use of energy. Lastly, renewable energy consumption reflects the intergenerational sustainability of economic growth (Dincer, 2000).

4.3.2 Social inclusion indicators[4]

Social inclusion can be defined as the process of improving citizen participation in socioeconomic activities, particularly for marginalised or disadvantaged groups. Enhancing inclusion can spur structural transformation by creating opportunities for these groups to enhance their productive capacities. Inequality is a powerful measure of social exclusion, however, the data and period coverage are very limited for several African countries.

An alternative proxy measure is unemployment rates. Low unemployment rates are a broad measure of inclusion. While this measure can also serve as a determinant of the poverty level (Jarvis and Jenkins, 1998), I acknowledge that employment can coexist with poverty when jobs are insecure and underemployment is prevalent.

In addition to unemployment, access to basic socioeconomic services such as sanitation provides an effective measure of social inclusion (Katukiza et al., 2010). In Sub-Saharan Africa, nearly 70 per cent of individuals do not have reliable access to basic sanitation services. I, therefore, use data on the share of the population with access to sanitation services as an additional proxy for social inclusion. The other indicators of social inclusion used are adolescent fertility rates and life expectancy.

Adolescent fertility rates are associated with maternal deaths and access to health services. According to the World Fertility Patterns report (UN, 2015), the average adolescent fertility rate in Africa over the period

1990–2015 was more than double the rate for all other continents except Latin America. High adolescent fertility rates undermine access to education, health and employment opportunities as unintended pregnancies adversely impact on maternal and child health, school drop-out rates and productivity, all of which contribute to higher poverty rates (Kibret, Bayu and Merga, 2014).

Life expectancy is associated with quality of life and has implications for social dynamics, including demographic transitions (ageing population), related changes in consumption patterns and industrial production dynamics. Life expectancy has indeed been widely applied to various globally accepted social development index formulations such as the Physical Quality of Life Index and the Human Development Index.[5]

4.3.3 Environmental conservation indicators[6]

Environmental hazards including those induced by climate change (e.g. floods, droughts and air pollution) can adversely affect output and productivity and thus undermine the transformation process through their destructive effects on infrastructure and the health of the citizenry. Enhancing resilience to climate change and environmental hazards can improve agricultural productivity and mitigate damages and losses stemming from environmental disasters. To capture the environmental factors that are likely to impact on structural change, this study uses carbon dioxide emissions (metric tonnes per capita), arable land (hectares per person), forest area and access to improved water sources as proxy indicators.

Carbon emissions tend to rise with industrial production, and hence, structural transformation. In the absence of appropriate technologies, initiatives to curb environmental degradation through the adoption of renewable energies can undermine industrial development by increasing production costs.

Environmental hazards such as floods and droughts negatively affect the number of people using improved water sources (Zander and Kächele, 1999). Meanwhile, water is an important input into energy production and consequently industrial output. Hence, limitations on access to water can have serious adverse consequences for industrial development. Access to water also influences industrial output through its impact on the agricultural sector, which is an important input into manufacturing.

Increased forest cover supports the planet's carbon sinks and is essential in sustaining Earth's ecosystem and strengthening its capacity to adapt to climate change (Foody, 2003). Efforts to curb deforestation, however, have obstructive implications for industrial activities that rely on wood-related inputs.

4.3.4 *Structural transformation indicator*[7]

To evaluate the impact of economic, social and environmental policy interventions on structural transformation, this study develops a composite index of structural transformation. The choice of indicators comprising the composite index is informed by the definitions of structural transformation discussed previously.

Shifts in sectoral shares are captured by the respective shares of manufacturing and service sector value-added (Christiaensen, Demery and Kuhl, 2011). Cereal yields per kilogram and gross agricultural output per capita are included in the index to reflect agricultural productivity. Indicators of technological (internet access per 100), financial sector development (domestic credit provided by financial sector, per cent of GDP) and human capital (infant mortality per 1,000 live births) development are all included to reflect broader aspects of structural transformation. Access to quality health services promotes social development and reflects the inclusiveness of the structural transformation process (Fayissa, 2001). Well-functioning financial markets facilitate the reallocation of economic resources and activities from low-productivity to high-productivity sectors (Wampah, 2013). The inclusion of technology indicators is justified on the grounds that technology and innovation facilitate structural transformation by enhancing factor productivity. The empirical evidence suggests that, across countries, structural transformation is associated with the adoption of capital-embodied technology (Araujo and Teixeira, 2010). Other studies have found that technology promotes inclusive development, via the diffusion of information and knowledge (Chang and Baek, 2010), while minimising the potentially negative effect of environmental degradation on human development (Asongu, le Roux and Biekpe, 2018).

4.4 Modelling approach

Based on 19 indicators,[8] this study adopts a structural equation modelling (SEM) approach, similar to the one employed by Spaiser et al. (2017), to evaluate the impact of social, economic and environmental interventions on structural transformation. However, unlike Spaiser et al., who investigated the trade-offs and synergies among socioeconomic and environmental indicators of sustainability, this study extends the analysis by exploring how the interactions among the dimensions of sustainable development influence the processes of structural transformation in Africa. Employing an SEM model allows us to estimate the direct and indirect effects of the three factors based on our path specifications (Schumacker and Lomax, 2004).

For this modelling technique, sample size requirements are controversial because complexity of models varies, thereby often relying on a traditional rule-of-thumb of: (1) a minimum sample size of 100; and (2) five observations per estimated parameter (MacCallum et al., 1999). Meanwhile, Wolf et al. (2013) applied a Monte Carlo simulation technique to determine the sample size requirements for SEM modelling in general. They investigated the parameter dynamics with respect to statistical power, bias of parameter estimates and overall solution of propriety and concluded a sample size requirement within a range from 30 to 460 and above to convey meaningful patterns of association under the SEM setting. More recently, however, Kline (2011) and Barrett (2007) recommended samples in number with at least 200, while depending on complexity of a model as well as other factors such as normality[9] of the data. Kline has further advanced a rule-of-thumb on the relationship between sample size and model complexity, which has empirically been supported by Jackson (2003) into namely, the N:q rule, the ratio of cases (N) to the estimated parameters (q). An ideal N:q rule is 20:1, while 10:1 at least ensures the trustworthiness of the results. Mindful of this, our study will employ 18 estimated parameters (discussed later) with 493 samples, satisfying the proposed sample requirements, while also acknowledging that our sample may not be large enough given the complexity of hypothetical models. Concerning the applicability of longitudinal design into the SEM setting, two modelling approaches could be used widely. The first is the latent growth curve modelling, which estimates two unobserved variables (an intercept and a slope) that permit them to have a different trajectory over time (Fan, 2003). Reflecting our modelling purposes (trade-offs and synergies), which would require an ability to control for unobserved, time-invariant, the second econometric approach should be more appropriate for our study, which is the fixed effect in the SEM setting (Bollen and Brand, 2008). Choice of estimation method is then important in this regard. Allison, Williams and Moral-Benito (2017) showed that this application is better estimated by employing maximum likelihood with the SEM software (ML-SEM). They have further demonstrated that the ML-SEM would have superior capability over others with respect to the handling of missing data and allowing for non-normal data.

In general, the two most commonly adopted methodologies of estimates of dependence in the SEM exercises are the maximum likelihood and the partial least squares (Maydeu-Olivares, 2017). The study benefits from a covariance approach by adopting the maximum likelihood specification because it is not only better suited for larger sample analysis but is also likely to be applicable to the analysis of a multivariate time-series in which the compositional data are transformed to follow the normal distribution (Crisci, 2012).

Specifically, this covariance-based SEM technique involves minimising the difference between observed and predicted variance-covariance matrices, which is based on the calculation of the covariance structure of the maximum likelihood method. It is also considered a relatively advanced approach that deals with unobserved heterogeneity whereas the partial least squares method appears to have limited control capacity, which further requires an extension of mixture regression (e.g. finite mixture partial least squares) (Becker et al., 2013).

In essence, the SEM exercise requires the validity of a measurement model before starting (Anderson and Gerbing, 1988). The measurement model uses confirmatory factor analysis to model the latent variables and then test the robustness of the model under hypothetical constructs. If the measurement model is statistically significant in its tests, I then move on to a structural equation model in order to quantify the direct and indirect relationships among the latent variables. The direct effects exclusively measure the independent impacts of economic, social and environmental interventions on structural transformation. The indirect effects take into account the interactions of each intervention with other interventions. The sum of these direct and indirect effects constitutes the total impact of each latent construct on structural transformation.

Our hypothetical model comprises four latent dimensions representing an index of structural transformation and its social, economic and environmental drivers. Each of the latent dimensions is explained by a group of sub-indicators. The four latent dimensions can be specified as:

$$\prod_{eco} \ni eco_{IJT}, \prod_{soc} \ni soc_{IJT}, \prod_{env} \ni env_{IJT}, \prod_{st} \ni st_{IJT}, \text{ for all I, J, T}$$

where i represents the observed indicators that comprise each of the latent variables ($i = 1,..., N$), j is country dimension ($j = 1,..., J$); t is time dimension ($t = 1,..., T$); eco is the latent economic dimension; soc is the latent social inclusion dimension; env is the latent environmental conservation dimension; st is the latent structural transformation proxy and $\prod$ simply identifies a variable as latent.

The following standardised regression coefficients are estimated:

$$\prod_{eco-soc}, \prod_{eco-env}, \prod_{eco-st}, \prod_{soc-eco}, \prod_{soc-env}, \prod_{soc-st},$$

$$\prod_{env-soc}, \prod_{env-eco} \text{ and } \prod_{env-st}$$

Where:

$\prod_{eco-soc}$ estimates the impact of economic growth interventions on social inclusion;

$\Pi_{eco\text{-}env}$ estimates the impact of economic growth interventions on environmental conservation;

$\Pi_{eco\text{-}st}$ measures the impact of economic growth interventions on structural transformation;

$\Pi_{soc\text{-}eco}$ measures the impact of social inclusion interventions on economic growth;

$\Pi_{soc\text{-}env}$ measures the impact of social inclusion interventions on environmental conservation;

$\Pi_{soc\text{-}st}$ represents the impact of social inclusion interventions on structural transformation;

$\Pi_{env\text{-}sco}$ estimates the impact of environmental conservation interventions on social inclusion;

$\Pi_{env\text{-}eco}$ measures the impact of environmental conservation interventions on economic growth; and

$\Pi_{env\text{-}st}$ is the impact of environmental conservation interventions on structural transformation.

Based on the latent and path specifications, the direct and indirect effects as well as total structural effects can be estimated as follows:

Total structural effects of economic growth interventions on structural transformation (I):

$$T_{eco\text{-}st} \ni \left\{ D_{eco\text{-}st}, I_{eco\text{-}st} \right\} = \left\{ \Pi_{eco\text{-}st}, \left(\Pi_{eco\text{-}soc} * \Pi_{soc\text{-}st} + \Pi_{eco\text{-}env} * \Pi_{env\text{-}st} \right) \right\},$$

Total structural effects of social inclusion interventions on structural transformation (II):

$$T_{soc\text{-}st} \ni \left\{ D_{soc\text{-}st}, I_{soc\text{-}st} \right\} = \left\{ \Pi_{soc\text{-}st}, \left(\Pi_{soc\text{-}eco} * \Pi_{eco\text{-}st} + \Pi_{soc\text{-}env} * \Pi_{env\text{-}st} \right) \right\},$$

Total structural effects of environmental conservation interventions on structural transformation (III):

$$T_{env\text{-}st} \ni \left\{ D_{env\text{-}st}, I_{env\text{-}st} \right\} = \left\{ \Pi_{env\text{-}st}, \left(\Pi_{env\text{-}eco} * \Pi_{eco\text{-}st} + \Pi_{env\text{-}soc} * \Pi_{soc\text{-}st} \right) \right\},$$

Where: T is the total structural effect, D is the direct effect, I is the indirect effect, which can further be measured by the sum of standardised regression weights of two different indirect pathways. There is a synergy effect if T > D or a trade-off effect if T < D.

Our three hypothetical models with the above-defined specifications are presented in Figure 4.2 and their analyses are conducted using SPSS-AMOS 23.

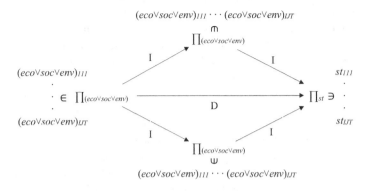

Figure 4.2 Hypothetical structural equation model.

4.5 Empirical results and discussions

Initially, the measurement model reveals that the relationships between the observed predictors and underlying constructs are statistically significant except for six indicators with coefficient values below 0.2 (per capita GDP in the economic growth construct, unemployment rate in the social inclusion construct, forest area in the environmental conservation construct and agriculture production index, internet users and infant mortality rate in the structural transformation construct). They are thus excluded from further analysis (Jöreskog, 1993).

The empirical results from our measurement model show that each of the standardised regression weights ($S\lambda$) exceed the critical value at the 0.01 significance level. In more detail, investment (0.327) and lower energy intensity levels (−0.648)[10] are estimated to have a positive impact on structural transformation. The results also highlight potential trade-offs (−0.790) between the renewable energy indicator and structural transformation in the African context, which is consistent with previous research (e.g. Armah and Baek, 2015; Spaiser et al., 2017). Regarding the social inclusion dimension, the provision of basic sanitation facilities (0.773), lower adolescent fertility rates (−0.784) and longer life expectancy (0.589) are all estimated to positively contribute to the process as expected (Kibret, Bayu and Merga, 2014; Armah and Baek, 2015). Meanwhile, the environment-related indicators reveal that increased carbon dioxide emissions (0.872) and improved access to water (0.803) will foster Africa's transformational initiative. However, arable land (−0.292) has a negative impact, which implies that industrialisation is associated with increased agricultural productivity and not the total size of available arable land.

However, having a significant reliability coefficient does not automatically guarantee an accurately measured construct (Hsu, Chen and Hsieh, 2006). Although there has been some development of the robustness testing methodology for the SEM, the most widely used three-step tests for assessing robustness are: (1) convergent validity; (2) discriminant validity; and (3) normal distribution of the data.

The first and arguably most essential of these is the test of convergent validity, which gives a critical understanding of the quality measures best designed to assess the level of correlation of multiple indicators of the same construct. In this context, each of the four constructs can then be confirmed by two types of tests for convergent validity: average variance extracted (AVE) and construct reliability (CR). As shown in Table 4.2, the AVEs for the four latent constructs far exceed the recommended level of 0.500 (Fornell and Larcker, 1981). In addition, the CR, which measures the extent to which the construct is free from random error, is computed to be: 0.882 for the economic construct; 0.792 for the social construct; 0.941 for the environmental construct; and 0.962 for the structural construct. All the values exceed the recommended threshold of 0.700, and hence, meet the reliability test (Bagozzi and Yi, 1988).

The second test is based on discriminant validity criteria, which can indicate the extent to which one construct is differing from another in an empirical manner, while also estimating the degree of difference among the

Table 4.2 Robustness test for measurement model: (1) convergent validity

	Λ^1	SE	CR^2	$S\lambda^3$	AVE^4	CR^5
Π_{eco}					0.87461	0.88208
Investment $_{jt}$	1	–	–	0.327		
Renewable energy $_{jt}$	−5.805	0.771	−7.525	−0.790		
Energy intensity $_{jt}$	−2.452	0.319	−7.697	−0.648		
Π_{soc}					0.94657	0.79151
Sanitation $_{jt}$	1	–	–	0.773		
Life expectancy $_{jt}$	0.153	0.011	13.740	0.589		
Adol. fertility $_{jt}$	−1.079	0.054	−20.081	−0.784		
Π_{env}					0.92548	0.94096
Acc. water $_{jt}$	1	–	–	0.803		
CO_2 emission $_{jt}$	5.362	0.245	21.881	0.872		
Arable land $_{jt}$	−0.586	0.092	−6.381	−0.292		
Π_{st}					0.86931	0.96219
Services VA $_{jt}$	1	–	–	0.420		
Cereal yield $_{jt}$	2.663	0.449	5.933	0.493		
Manufacturing VA $_{jt}$	2.998	0.343	8.730	0.625		
Domestic credit $_{jt}$	6.880	1.038	6.628	0.735		

Notes: 1 = factor loading; 2 = construct reliability of each indicator; 3 = standardised factor loading; 4 = average variance extracted, computed based on $\sum S\lambda^2 / (\sum S\lambda^2 + \sum$ variance); 5 = construct reliability of each construct, computed based on $(\sum S\lambda)^2 / [(\sum S\lambda)^2 + \sum$ variance].

overlapping constructs. In this regard, the results of the discriminant validity test should meet the two specific criteria as follows.

One of the criteria is that the AVE for the four latent constructs must be greater than any squared value of the correlation coefficient, which can be evaluated by using cross-loading of indicators, known as the Fornell and Larcker criterion (Henseler, Ringle and Sarstedt, 2015). Table 4.3 shows that the largest squared value of the correlation coefficients is 0.26214, which falls between the social and structural transformation constructs. In other words, the square root of each construct's AVE (calculated in Table 4.2) has a greater value than any correlation with other latent constructs, meeting criterion of a latent construct being able to explain better the variance of its own variable rather than the variance of other latent constructs.

The other criterion is that the range between calculated values of the correlation coefficient (calculated by subtracting and adding the product of 1.96 and the associated standard error [SE]) must not include the value of 1 (Streukens and Leroi-Werelds, 2016). Meeting this criterion confirms that bootstrap confidence intervals with SEM derive from a precise calculation of the quantiles for the middle 95 per cent of a perfect normal distribution, which is the case for our measurement modelling results. In particular, the result of bootstrap confidence is critical and should be statistically valid when it comes to evaluating indirect effects. In other words, the validity of standardised indirect effects can only be evaluated based on a two-tailed bootstrap significance test (Li, Kang and Haney, 2017).

Theoretically speaking in the SEM setting, non-normality of the sample data leads to an overestimation of the chi-squared statistic, thereby potentially resulting in false rejection of the model. A normality check is thus

Table 4.3 Robustness test for measurement model: (2) discriminant validity

Correlations	Π_{eco}	Π_{soc}	Π_{env}	Π_{st}
Π_{eco}	1			
Π_{soc}	0.01823	1		
Π_{env}	0.14288	0.01988	1	
Π_{st}	0.06760	0.26214	0.15840	1
Bootstrap Intervals	*SE*	*−1.96*	*+1.96*	*P-value*
$\Pi_{eco} \leftrightarrow \Pi_{soc}$	0.003	0.1291	0.1409	0.004
$\Pi_{eco} \leftrightarrow \Pi_{env}$	0.001	0.3760	0.3800	0.004
$\Pi_{eco} \leftrightarrow \Pi_{st}$	0.001	0.2580	0.2625	0.008
$\Pi_{soc} \leftrightarrow \Pi_{env}$	0.002	0.1371	0.1449	0.004
$\Pi_{soc} \leftrightarrow \Pi_{st}$	0.001	0.5100	0.5140	0.004
$\Pi_{env} \leftrightarrow \Pi_{st}$	0.000	0.3970	0.3990	0.004

Note: Bootstrapping is a process of re-sampling the existing data set using the method of sampling with replacement.

required in which the values of the skewness tend to be well-controlled (Gao, Mokhtarian and Johnston, 2008). A rule-of-thumb in this normality assessment is that, in general, an absolute value of skewness lower than 2.0 means the data is normally distributed (George and Mallery, 2010). However, the maximum likelihood estimator for the SEM exercise is likely robust to skewness for cases greater than 2.0 (absolute value) if an absolute critical value does not exceed ten in general (Awang, 2015). In this context, our data is acceptable in terms of either normality or moderate non-normality (Table 4.4).

Since the measurement model is confirmed by the above validity tests, we now move on to specifying our hypothetical SEM models. The empirical results from the three hypothetical models presented in Figures 4.3, 4.4 and 4.5 illustrate three development scenarios. The first model represents a structural transformation agenda that is driven by economic growth interventions. The second depicts a structural transformation process that prioritises social inclusion-driven development while the third prioritises environmental considerations. All three models estimate the direct and indirect impacts of the three dimensions of sustainable development on structural transformation in Africa. The *t*-values of all standardised regression weights for all three models are statistically significant. In so doing, we conduct modification indices techniques to improve the model fit if residuals (i.e. *e*1 through *e*13) among indicator variables are allowed to correlate (Barrett, 2007).

In Model I, the direct effect of economic growth on structural transformation is estimated at 1.091 (i.e. the standardised regression weight), which implies that structural transformation improves by 1.091 standard deviations when measures to improve economic growth increase by one standard

Table 4.4 Robustness test for measurement model: (3) normal distribution

Variables	Min	Max	Skewness	Critical value
Investment $_{jt}$	0.40	1.70	−1.087	−7.851
Renewable energy $_{jt}$	−0.70	2.00	−1.830	−9.650
Energy intensity $_{jt}$	0.40	1.60	0.160	1.450
Sanitation $_{jt}$	0.70	2.00	−0.007	−0.065
Life expectancy $_{jt}$	1.60	1.90	0.395	3.581
Adol. fertility $_{jt}$	0.80	2.30	−2.019	−8.298
Acc. water $_{jt}$	1.50	2.00	−0.119	−1.074
CO_2 emission $_{jt}$	−1.30	1.00	0.584	5.296
Arable land $_{jt}$	0.03	1.49	2.626	9.864
Services VA $_{jt}$	1.11	1.83	−1.523	−13.804
Cereal yield $_{jt}$	2.12	3.88	−0.013	−0.117
Manufacturing VA $_{jt}$	0.35	1.34	−0.595	−5.390
Domestic credit $_{jt}$	−0.44	2.28	−0.550	−4.985

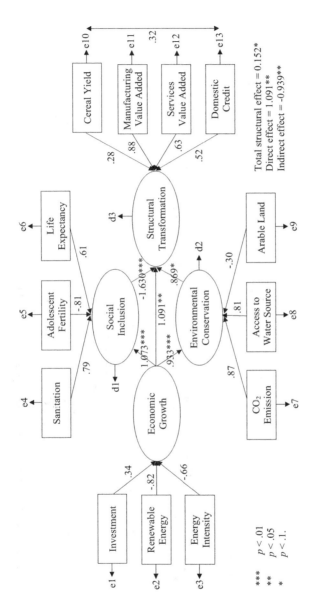

Figure 4.3 Results of parsimonious structural equation model I.

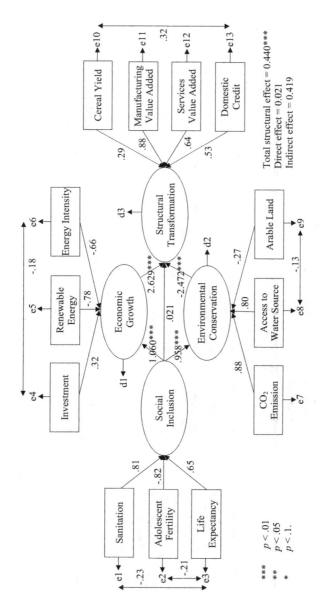

Figure 4.4 Results of parsimonious structural equation model II.

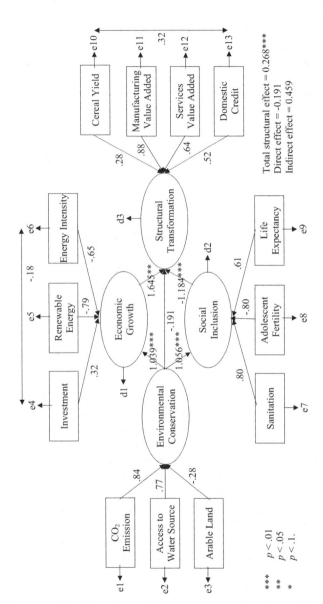

Figure 4.5 Results of parsimonious structural equation model III.

deviation (see Figure 4.3). But the results also indicate that there are two indirect effects: one is through the social inclusion dimension and the other effect is through the environmental conservation dimension.

The first indirect pathway reveals that the impact of economic growth on structural transformation reduces when such efforts are accompanied by efforts to improve social inclusion. Specifically, social inclusion interventions reduce the direct impact of economic measures by approximately −1.749 standard deviations.[11] Similarly, economic interventions that are mediated by environmental considerations tend to have a weaker, yet positive, impact (i.e. 0.811 standard deviations[12]) on structural transformation than the direct effect. Nevertheless, this impact is greater than interventions mediated by social sustainability considerations. Cumulatively, the two indirect effects totalling −0.939 standard deviations, reduce the direct effect of 1.091 to a mere 0.152 (a decline of ~86 per cent).

Models II and III follow the same estimation logic. Model II reflects a scenario where structural transformation is driven by social development priorities. It shows that social interventions have a positive but relatively weak direct effect of 0.021 on structural transformation (see Figure 4.4). However, this outcome is leveraged when it is accompanied by measures to improve economic growth (2.787 standard deviations[13]). Trade-offs are however observed when social inclusion interventions are mediated by environmental conservation objectives (−2.368 standard deviations[14]). Nonetheless, on net, the negative environmental conservation effect is offset by the positive economic growth effect resulting in a total effect of 0.440 (i.e. a net indirect effect of 0.419 and a direct effect of 0.021).

Unlike Models I and II, Model III reveals that environmental conservation programmes have a negative direct effect of −0.191 on structural transformation but this negative effect is reversed to 0.269 standard deviations (by 245 per cent) when such measures are accompanied by economic growth (1.709[15]) and social inclusion (−1.250[16]) interventions (see Figure 4.5). Conceivably, environmental conservation interventions boost economic growth by spurring investments in renewable energy and improving efficiencies in energy use. However, social interventions further reduce the environmental conservation impact by −1.250, resulting in the total indirect effect of 0.459. The negative social effects of environmental conservation interventions may reflect the tensions between the objective of maintaining "ecological wilderness" and satisfying the resource needs of local communities.

The above interpretations of the modelling results should further be supported by evaluating model-fit indices to test whether the above three models can reflect underlying theory. The following two categories of model-fit indices are widely agreed as having the best interpretive value in assessing model fit: (1) absolute fit indices; and (2) incremental fit indices (McDonald and Ho, 2002). Absolute fit indices provide the most fundamental indication of how well our hypothetical models fit the sample data. For this purpose, this category has four most widely reported fit indices (Hooper, Coughlan and Mullen, 2008): the chi-square (χ^2); the goodness-of-fit index (GFI); root-mean-square residual (RMR); and standardised root-mean-square residual (SRMR).

The χ^2 value is considered the conventional measure for assessing overall model fit by calculating the magnitude of discrepancy between the data and fitted covariance matrices (Hu and Bentler, 1999). Although we can confirm all estimated χ^2 values are statistically significant, they may not, however, provide further detailed assessment information. That is why an alternative test is necessary, namely the GFI, which can indicate how our models come close to replicating the observed covariance matrix. For this index, our model exceeds the minimum model-fit cut-off value of 0.7 or above (Tabachnick and Fidell, 2007).

Meanwhile, the RMR, the square root of the difference between the residuals of the covariance matrix and the hypothesised covariance model, is also considered for this purpose but it is somewhat difficult to interpret. On the other hand, the SRMR is preferred in terms of ease of interpretation. A value of the SRMR as high as 0.08 is deemed acceptable, although a value of less than 0.07 is considered well-fitting (Diamantopoulos and Siguaw, 2000).

Another critical group of measures is the incremental fit indices, mostly composed of the normed fit index (NFI) and the comparative fit index (CFI) (Miles and Shevlin, 2007). The NFI compares the estimated χ^2 value from our models with that of the null model (the worst scenario that assumes all measured variables are uncorrelated). Traditionally, values greater than 0.80 were interpreted as very good fits but this traditional guideline has been criticised because the NFI value can be quite sensitive to sample size and even the cut-off point (0.80) remains controversial among SEM modellers.

An alternative to the NFI is the CFI, which is not sensitive to sample size (Tabachnick and Fidell, 2007). Similar to the NFI, it assumes that all latent constructs are uncorrelated and so compares the sample covariance with the null model. In fact, there is no clear cut-off value in this measure but a value greater than 0.70 is preferred. As shown in Table 4.5, the models employed in the study meet the test of fitness criteria regardless of the category of model-fit index adopted.

Table 4.5 Summary of model-fit indices for structural equation models

	Absolute fit indices				Incremental fit indices	
	χ^2	GFI	RMR	SRMR	NFI	CFI
Model I	805.420***	0.815	0.009	0.0944	0.769	0.781
Model II	753.322***	0.825	0.009	0.0920	0.784	0.795
Model III	811.047***	0.819	0.009	0.0937	0.767	0.779

Notes: χ^2 = chi-square; GFI = goodness-of-fit index; RMR = root-mean-square residual; SRMR = standard root-mean-square residual; NFI = normed fit index; CFI = comparative fit index; *** $p < 0.01$; ** $p < 0.05$; and * $p < 0.1$.

4.6 Concluding remarks

In short, this chapter investigated synergies and trade-offs among the economic, social and environmental drivers of structural transformation and examined how these factors in turn impact on structural transformation in Africa. The chapter contributes in this regard to the literature by identifying the appropriate sequencing of policies to achieve structural transformation in Africa and quantifying the direct and indirect impact of environmental, social and economic policy interventions on structural transformation.

I have found that indicators of social development (compared with those of economic and environmental development) tend to have the greatest total impact on structural transformation even though the direct effects of such indicators tend to be relatively weak. On the other hand, indicators of economic growth have the weakest total effects even though they have the largest direct impact. In contrast, environmentally driven development programmes have negative direct impacts on structural transformation, but their total impact is positive and higher than the economically driven approach but lower than the socially driven approach.

In particular, our findings have a number of important policy implications for the field of development planning. Notwithstanding valid concerns of policymakers about the trade-offs associated with environmentally driven development agendas, the empirical results show that the total contribution of environmental initiatives to Africa's structural transformation agenda (Model III) is greater than that of a structural transformation agenda that is led by economic growth strategies (Model I).

It is important to note that the findings do not suggest that a successful structural transformation programme requires an exclusive focus on the social dimension. What it does suggest is that a structural transformation initiative led by social development is more catalytic in terms of its impact. This implies that prioritising social development in most African countries may be the most expeditious pathway to achieving structural transformation. Thus, this study provides policymakers with a useful framework for prioritising and sequencing policy interventions to achieve a global agenda for sustainable development and advance their structural transformation objectives. With this in mind, there are several areas ripe for future research that can build on this study. Our study raises the important question of whether the findings are robust to individual country contexts. By answering this question, more concrete guidelines will be provided to countries that are in the process of implementing the SDGs and this will constitute an important step in making structural transformation a sustainable and operational reality in Africa. Furthermore, to the extent that the study is largely driven by outcome variables, including policy variables in the models could strengthen the policy relevance of the findings. Finally, access to data on a broader range of indicators would enhance the quality and robustness of the latent constructs used in this study.

Notes

1 They are Algeria, Angola, Botswana, Burkina Faso, Cameroon, Cote d'Ivoire, Egypt, Gabon, the Gambia, Ghana, Guinea, Guinea-Bissau, Kenya, Madagascar, Malawi, Mali, Morocco, Mozambique, Namibia, Niger, Nigeria, Senegal, Sierra Leone, South Africa, United Republic of Tanzania, Togo, Tunisia, Uganda and Zambia.

2 Economic growth has four selected areas of importance: output (proxied by annual growth rates of per capita GDP from the WDI); investment (proxied by total investment as per cent of GDP from the WEO); green economy (proxied by renewable energy consumption as a share of the total energy consumption from the WDI); and energy use (proxied by energy intensity level of primary energy from the WDI).

3 GDP per capita is admittedly a controversial indicator of well-being. Despite its merit as a widely used measure of economic performance across countries, it can be a misleading metric since it tells us little about the utility of the goods and services produced by a country. For instance, going to war increases GDP and destroying infrastructure and re-building it also increases GDP. Alternative measures of well-being include the Genuine Progress Indicator and "Beyond GDP" under the System of Environmental-Economic Accounts. For the purpose of this study, it would be hard to see clearly the trade-offs or synergies between social inclusion and economic growth (using the Genuine Progress Indicator), and between environmental conservation and economic growth (using "Beyond GDP" indicator) since these two indicators tend to be multi-dimensional in nature. Most importantly, the lack of data availability in these relatively new measures remains a challenge in Africa. In fact, the per capita GDP indicator is ultimately excluded from the analysis since it is not statistically significant in the measurement model.

4 Social inclusion has four selected areas of importance: poverty (proxied by unemployment rate from the WDI); sanitation (proxied the share of population with access to sanitation facilities from the WDI); life quality (proxied by the

number of years of life expectancy from the WDI); and maternal health (proxied by adolescent fertility rate at births per 1,000 women ages 15–19 from the WDI).

5 The Physical Quality of Life Index is an equally weighted measure of well-being. It is based on the following: the basic literacy rate; infant mortality; and life expectancy. The Human Development Index (HDI) is a composite index of life expectancy, education and income per capita. A variant of the HDI is the inequality-adjusted Human Development Index, regularly published by the United Nations Development Programme. These are the two most popular measures of social development, particularly emphasising human physical performance as a core element (Ray, 2008).

6 Environmental conservation has four selected areas of importance: climate change (proxied by emissions of carbon dioxide at metric tons per capita from the WDI); agricultural land (proxied by arable land at hectares per person; WDI); forest cover (proxied by forest area (square km); WDI); and water (proxied by the share of population with access to improved water sources; WDI).

7 Structural transformation has five selected areas of importance: agriculture (proxied by cereal yield kg per hectare from the WDI and by per capita gross agricultural production index from the FAO); manufacturing (proxied by manufacturing value-added as a per cent of GDP from the WDI); ICT (proxied by services value-added as a per cent of GDP and by internet users per 100 people from the WDI); health (proxied by infant mortality rate per 1,000 live births from the WDI); and financial market (proxied by domestic credit provided by financial sector as a per cent of GDP from the WDI).

8 Thirteen of the 19 indicators are used to construct the social, economic and environmental drivers of structural transformation and they are transformed into the natural logarithm for modelling that shows a positive skew to normalise their distributions.

9 This will be explored in a detail later during measurement model analysis.

10 A lower ratio of energy intensity indicates that less energy is used to produce one unit of output.

11 This is calculated by multiplying the two indirect effects (i.e. 1.073 by −1.630).

12 This is calculated by multiplying the two indirect effects (i.e. 0.933 by 0.869).

13 This is calculated by multiplying the two indirect effects (i.e. 1.060 by 2.629).

14 This is calculated by multiplying the two indirect effects (i.e. 0.958 by −2.472).

15 This is calculated by multiplying the two indirect effects (i.e. 1.039 by 1.645).

16 This is calculated by multiplying the two indirect effects (i.e. 1.056 by −1.184).

References

Allison, P.D., Williams, R. and Moral-Benito, E., 2017. Maximum likelihood for cross-lagged panel models with fixed effects, socius. *Sociological Research for a Dynamic World*, 3, pp.1–17.

Anderson, J.C. and Gerbing, D.W., 1988. Structural equation modelling in practice: A review and recommended two-step approach. *Psychological Bulletin*, 103(3), pp.411–423.

Araujo, R.S.A. and Teixeira, J.R., 2010. Investment specific technological progress and structural change. *Estudos Econômicos*, 40(4), pp.819–829.

Armah, B. and Baek, S.J., 2015. Can the SDGs promote structural transformation in Africa? An empirical analysis. *Development*, 58(4), pp.473–491.

Armah, B. and Baek, S.J., 2018. Three interventions to foster sustainable transformation in Africa. *Journal of Social, Political and Economic Studies*, 43(1–2), pp.3–25.

Armah, B., Keita, M., Gueye, A., Bosco, V., Ameso, J. and Chinzara, Z., 2014. Structural transformation for inclusive development in Africa: The role of active government policies. *Development*, 57(3–4), pp.438–451.

Asongu, S.A., le Roux, S. and Biekpe, N., 2018. Enhancing ICT for environmental sustainability in Sub-Saharan Africa. *Technological Forecasting and Social Change*, 127, pp.209–216.

AUC (African Union Commission), 2015. Agenda 2063: *The Africa we want. A shared strategic framework for inclusive growth and sustainable development.* Addis Ababa: AUC.

Awang, Z., 2015. *SEM made simple: A gentle approach to learning structural equation modelling.* Selangor, Malaysia: MPWS Rich Publication Sdn. Bhd.

Baek, S.J., 2017. Is rising income inequality far from inevitable during structural transformation? A proposal for an augmented inequality dynamics. *Journal of Economics and Political Economy*, 4(3), pp.224–237.

Baek, S.J., 2018. *The Political Economy of Neo-modernisation: Rethinking the dynamics of technology, development and inequality.* London: Palgrave Macmillan.

Baek, S.J., 2019. Cooperating in Africa's sustainable structural transformation: Policymaking capacity and the role of emerging economies. *International Development Planning Review*, 41(4), pp.419–434.

Bagozzi, R.P. and Yi, Y., 1988. On the evaluation of structural equation models. *Journal of the Academy of Marketing Science*, 16, pp.74–94.

Banerjee, A.V. and Newman, A.F., 1993. Occupational choice and the process of development. *Journal of Political Economy*, 101(2), pp.274–298.

Barrett, P., 2007. Structural equation modelling: Adjudging model fit. *Personality and Individual Differences*, 42, pp.815–824.

Basu, P. and Guariglia, A., 2008. Education and industrialization. *Southern Economic Journal*, 75(1), pp.104–127.

Becker, J.M., Rai, A., Ringle, C.M., and Völckner, F., 2013. Discovering unobserved heterogeneity in structural equation models to avert validity threats. *MIS Quarterly*, 37(3), pp.665–694.

Bollen, K.A. and Brand, J.E., 2008. *Fixed and random effects in panel data using structural equations models*, California Center for Population Research (PWP-CCPR-2008-003), Los Angeles, CA: University of California.

Chang, Y.S. and Baek, S.J., 2010. Limit to improvement: Myth or reality? Empirical analysis of historical improvement on three technologies influential in the evolution of civilization. *Technological Forecasting and Social Change*, 77(5), pp.712–729.

Christiaensen, L., Demery, L. and Kuhl, J., 2011. The (evolving) role of agriculture in poverty reduction: An empirical perspective. *Journal of Development Economics*, 98(2), pp.239–254.

Collier, P. and Venables, A.J., 2012. Greening Africa? Technologies, endowments and the latecomer effect. *Energy Economics*, 34, pp.S75–S84.

Crisci, A., 2012. Estimation methods for the structural equation models: Maximum likelihood, partial least squares and generalized maximum entropy. *Journal of Applied Quantitative Methods*, 7(2), pp.3–17.

Dastidar, A.G., 2012. Income distribution and structural transformation: Empirical evidence from developed and developing countries. *Seoul Journal of Economics*, 25(1), pp.25–52.

de la Croix, D. and Doepke, M., 2003. Inequality and growth: Why differential fertility matters. *American Economic Review*, 93(4), pp.1091–1113.

Deaton, A., 2013. *The Great Escape: Health, Wealth, and the Origins of Inequality.* Princeton, NJ: Princeton University Press.

Deutsch, J. and Silber, J., 2004. Measuring the impact of various income sources on the link between inequality and development: Implications for the Kuznets curve. *Review of Development Economics*, 8(1), pp.110–127.

Diamantopoulos, A. and Siguaw, J.A., 2000. *Introducing LISREL.* London: Sage Publications.

Dincer, I., 2000. Renewable energy and sustainable development: A crucial review. *Renewable and Sustainable Energy Reviews*, 4(2), pp.157–175.

ECA (Economic Commission for Africa), AUC, AfDB (African Development Bank) and UNDP (United Nations Development Programme), 2016. *MDGs to agenda 2063/SDGs transition report 2016: Towards an integrated and coherent approach to sustainable development in Africa.* Addis Ababa: ECA.

Elliott, D.R., 1998. Does growth cause structural transformation? Evidence from Latin America and the Caribbean. *Journal of Developing Areas*, 32, pp.187–198.

Fan, X., 2003. Power of latent growth modeling for detecting group differences in linear growth trajectory parameters. *Structural Equation Modeling*, 10, pp.380–400.

FAO (Food and Agriculture Organization), 2016. *FAO statistics division database* [Online]. Rome: FAO. Available from: http://faostat3.fao.org [Accessed 5 April 2016].

Fayissa, B., 2001. The determinants of infant and child mortality in developing countries: The case of Sub-Sahara Africa. *Review of Black Political Economy*, 29, pp.83–100.

Foody, G.M., 2003. Remote sensing of tropical forest environments: Towards the monitoring of environmental resources for sustainable development. *International Journal of Remote Sensing*, 24(20), pp.4035–4046.

Fornell, C. and Larcker, D., 1981. Evaluating structural equation models with unobservable variables and measurement error. *Journal of Marketing Research*, 18, pp.39–50.

Gao, S., Mokhtarian, P. and Johnston, R., 2008. Nonnormality of data in structural equation models. *Transportation Research Record: Journal of the Transportation Research Board*, 2416, pp.27–36.

George, D. and Mallery, M., 2010. *SPSS for windows step by step: A simple guide and reference* (17.0 update). Boston, MA: Pearson.

Giddings, B., Hopwood, B. and O'Brien, G., 2002. Environment, economy and society: Fitting them together into sustainable development. *Sustainable Development*, 10, pp.187–196.

Henseler, J., Ringle, C.M., and Sarstedt, M., 2015. A new criterion for assessing discriminant validity in variance-based structural equation modeling. *Journal of the Academy of Marketing Science*, 43(1), pp.115–135.

Herrendorf, B., Rogerson, R. and Valentinyi, Á., 2013. Two perspectives on preferences and structural transformation. *American Economic Review*, 103(7), pp.2752–2789.

Hooper, D., Coughlan, J. and Mullen, M.R., 2008. Structural equation modelling: Guidelines for determining model fit. *Electronic Journal of Business Research Methods*, 6(1), pp.53–60.

Hsu, S.H., Chen, W.H. and Hsieh, M.J., 2006. Robustness testing of PLS, LISREL, EQS and ANN-based SEM for measuring customer satisfaction. *Total Quality Management*, 17(3), pp.355–371.

Hu, L.T. and Bentler, P.M., 1999. Cutoff criteria for fit indexes in covariance structure analysis: Conventional criteria versus new alternatives. *Structural Equation Modeling*, 6(1), pp.1–55.

IMF (International Monetary Fund), 2016. *World economic outlook database* [Online], Washington, DC: IMF. Available from: http://www.imf.org/external/ns /cs.aspx?id=28 [Accessed 5 April 2016].

Jackson, D.L., 2003. Revisiting sample size and number of parameter estimates: Some support for the N:q hypothesis. *Structural Equation Modeling*, 10, pp.128–141.

Jarvis, S. and Jenkins, S., 1998. How much income mobility is there in Britain? *The Economic Journal*, 108(447), pp.428–443.

Jöreskog, K.G., 1993. *Testing structural equation models*. Sage focus ed. Thousand Oaks, CA: Sage Publications.

Katukiza, A.Y., Ronteltap, M., Oleja, A., Niwagaba, C.B., Kansiime, F. and Lens, P.N.L., 2010. Selection of sustainable sanitation technologies for urban slums: A case of Bwaise III in Kampala, Uganda. *Science of the Total Environment*, 409, pp.52–62.

Kibret, A., Bayu, H. and Merga, M., 2014. Prevalence of unintended pregnancy and associated factors among pregnant women attending antenatal clinics in Debre-markos Town, North West Ethiopia 2012. *Journal of Women's Health*, 4(3), pp.1–6.

Kline, R.B., 2011. *Principles and Practice of Structural Equation Modeling*. New York: Guilford Press.

Kuznets, S., 1955. Economic growth and income inequality. *American Economic Review*, 49, pp.1–28.

Li, S., Kang, M. and Haney, M.H., 2017. The effect of supplier development on outsourcing performance: The mediating roles of opportunism and flexibility. *Production Planning and Control*, 28(6–8), pp.599–609.

López-Menéndez, A.J., Pérez, R. and Moreno, B., 2014. Environmental costs and renewable energy: Re-visiting the environmental Kuznets curve. *Journal of Environmental Management*, 145(1), pp.368–373.

MacCallum, R.C., Widaman, K.F., Zhang, S. and Hong, S., 1999. Sample size in factor analysis. *Psychological Methods*, 4, pp.84–99.

Martorano, B., Park, D. and Sanfilippo, M., 2017. Catching-up, structural transformation, and inequality: Industry-level evidence from Asia. *Industrial and Corporate Change*, 26(4), pp.555–570.

Maydeu-Olivares, A., 2017. Maximum likelihood estimation of structural equation models for continuous data: Standard errors and goodness of fit. *Structural Equation Modeling: A Multidisciplinary Journal*, 24, pp.383–394.

McDonald, R.P. and Ho, M., 2002. Principles and practice in reporting statistical equation analyses. *Psychological Methods*, 7(1), pp.64–82.

Mijiyawa, A.G., 2017. Drivers of structural transformation: The case of the manufacturing sector in Africa. *World Development*, 99, pp.141–159.

Miles, J. and Shevlin, M., 2007. A time and a place for incremental fit indices. *Personality and Individual Differences*, 42(5), pp.869–874.

Moscona, J., 2018. *Agricultural development and structural change within and across countries*. MIT Department of Economics Working Paper. Available from: http://economics.mit.edu/files/13482.

Nurkse, R., 1953. *Problems of capital formation in underdeveloped countries*. New York: Oxford University Press.

Osman, R.H., Alexiou, C. and Tsaliki, P., 2012. The role of institutions in economic development: Evidence from 27 Sub-Saharan African countries. *International Journal of Social Economics*, 39(1/2), pp142–160.

Piketty, T., 1997. The dynamics of the wealth distribution and the interest rate with credit rationing. *Review of Economic Studies*, 64(2), pp.173–189.

Qizilbash, M., 2010. Sustainable development: Concepts and rankings. *Journal of Development Studies*, 37(3), pp.134–161.

Ray, A.K., 2008. Measurement of social development: An international comparison. *Social Indicators Research*, 86, pp.1–46.

Restuccia, D. and Rogerson, R., 2017. The causes and costs of misallocation. *Journal of Economic Perspectives*, 31(3), pp.151–174.

Schumacker, R.E., and Lomax, R.G., 2004. *A beginner's guide to structural equation modelling*. New Jersey: Lawrence Erlbaum Associates.

Shen, J., Dunn, D. and Shen, Y., 2007. Challenges facing U.S. manufacturing and strategies. *Journal of Industrial Technology*, 23(2), pp.2–10.

Simon, D., 2013. Climate and environmental change and the potential for greening African cities. *Local Economy*, 28(2), pp.203–217.

Spaiser, V., Ranganathan, S., Swain, R.B. and Sumpter, D.J.T., 2017. The sustainable development oxymoron: Quantifying and modelling the incompatibility of sustainable development goals. *International Journal of Sustainable Development and World Ecology*, 24(6), pp.457–470.

Sposi, M., 2019. Evolving comparative advantage, sectoral linkages, and structural change. *Journal of Monetary Economics*, 103, pp.75–87.

Stiglitz, J.E., 1996. Some lessons from the East Asian miracle. *World Bank Research Observer*, 11(2), pp.151–177.

Streukens, S. and Leroi-Werelds, S., 2016. Bootstrapping and PLS-SEM: A step-by-step guide to get more out of your bootstrap results. *European Management Journal*, 34, pp.618–632.

Swiecki, T., 2017. Determinants of structural change. *Review of Economic Dynamics*, 24(1), pp.95–131.

Tabachnick, B.G. and Fidell, L.S., 2007. *Using multivariate statistics*. 5th ed. New York: Allyn and Bacon.

Teignier, M., 2018. The role of trade in structural transformation. *Journal of Development Economics*, 130(C), pp.45–65.

Timmer, C.P., 2017. Food security, structural transformation, markets and government policy. *Asia & the Pacific Policy Studies*, 4(1), pp.4–19.

UN (United Nations), 2015. *World fertility patterns 2015*. New York: UN.

UN, 2019. *Global sustainable development report 2019: The future is now: Science for achieving sustainable development*. New York: UN.

UNCTAD (United Nations Conference on Trade and Development), 2016. *UNCTADstat* [Online]. Geneva: UNCTAD. Available from: http://unctadstat .unctad.org [Accessed 7 June 2016].

UNCTAD, 2018. *The least developed countries report 2018: Entrepreneurship for structural transformation: Beyond business as usual*. Geneva: UNCTAD.

Ungor, M., 2017. Productivity growth and labor reallocation: Latin America versus East Asia. *Review of Economic Dynamics*, 24, pp.25–42.

UNSD (United Nations Statistics Division), 2016. *Millennium development goals database* [Online]. New York: UN. Available from: http://mdgs.un.org/unsd/ mdg/default.aspx [Accessed 7 June 2016].

Vera, I. and Langlois, L., 2007. Energy indicators for sustainable development. *Energy*, 32(6), pp.875–882.

Wampah, H.A.K., 2013. What does it take to build a stable and efficient financial sector for sustaining growth and structural transformation in Africa? In: D. Willem te Velde and S. Griffith-Jones, eds. *Sustaining growth and structural transformation in Africa: how can a stable and efficient financial sector help?* London: Overseas Development Institute.

Wolf, E.J., Harrington, K.M., Clark, S.L. and Miller, M.W., 2013. Sample size requirements for structural equation models: An evaluation of power, bias, and solution propriety. *Educational and Psychological Measurement*, 76(6), pp.913–934.

World Bank, 2016. *World development indicators* [Online]. Washington, DC: World Bank. Available from: http://data.worldbank.org/data-catalog/world -development-indicators [Accessed 7 June 2016].

Zander, P. and Kächele, H., 1999. Modelling multiple objectives of land use for sustainable development. *Agricultural Systems*, 55, pp.311–325.

5 An integrated approach to shaping the future we want

5.1 Summary of the key findings

I began this study by trying to answer one central question, underpinned by two sub-questions as follows:

In answering the first sub-question, "How do empirical trade-offs and synergies between economic growth, social inclusion and environmental conservation affect structural transformation outcomes?" I built three models employing the structural equation modelling approach: the first represents a structural transformation agenda that is driven by economic growth interventions; the second depicts a structural transformation process that prioritises social inclusion-driven development; and the third prioritises environmental considerations. The modelling results suggest that the indicators of social development tend to have the greatest total influence (relationship) on a composite indicator of structural transformation (see Box 5.1) even though the direct effects of such indicators would appear to be relatively weak. Meanwhile, indicators of economic growth have the weakest total effects even though they have the largest direct relationship. In contrast, environmentally driven development programmes have a negative direct relationship to structural transformation, with their total relationship being positive and higher than the economic driven approach but lower than with the socially driven one.

These trade-offs and synergy investigations can be further supported by the results from a panel data econometric study conducted by Armah and Baek (2015). Their modelling results showed that when the economic and social dimensions are ignored, structural transformation is associated with statistically significant emissions of carbon dioxide, while an integrated approach also minimises trade-offs between transformation and environmental preservation. Their findings have also revealed synergies between transformation and adolescent fertility rates as well as transformation and access to social services such as sanitation. In this context, the most

DOI: 10.4324/9781003259916-5

important insights gained from their modelling exercise were that an inclusive and sustainable structural transformation agenda requires tackling the economic, social and environmental dimensions of sustainable development in an integrated way, which is in line with my arguments based on the structural equation modelling.

The next question, "What policy measures maximise the synergies to promote structural transformation in line with inclusive sustainable development?" was then addressed by the evidence documented in the analysis of potential trade-offs in achieving the triple objectives of economic growth, social equity and environmental sustainability. Moreover, the empirical evidence has underscored the role of proactive government policies (i.e. institutional capacity for development planning) in leveraging synergies among the three dimensions of sustainable development to advance the process of structural transformation. Building on the New Structural Economics perspectives on structural transformation,[1] I propose three catalytic and mutually reinforcing areas of intervention that can advance sustainable structural transformation in Africa by prioritising investments in renewable energy, human capital and financial inclusion.

My answers to these sub-questions contribute to addressing the overarching research question of the book, "What is the nature of the relationship between 'inclusive sustainable development' and 'structural transformation' with particular reference to low-income countries?" Their combined theoretical and practical contributions are brought together through discussion of the Inclusive Sustainable Development (ISD) framework, which also leads to suggestions for potential areas of future study to further enrich this field of research.

BOX 5.1 MEASURING THE MULTI-DIMENSIONAL INDEX OF STRUCTURAL TRANSFORMATION

Measuring structural transformation remains controversial as it is considered new development thinking as a process- and outcome-driven context-dependent national development priority for a majority of developing countries (Dabla-Norris et al., 2013). Traditionally, it has been defined as a process by which the relative importance of different sectors and activities of an economy change over time, particularly sectoral share from agriculture to industry and services (Herrendorf, Rogerson and Valentinyi, 2013), while also improving agricultural productivity (Christiaensen, Demery and Kuhl, 2011). These shifts in sectoral shares can be captured by the respective shares of manufacturing and service sectors value-added, whereas agricultural productivity can be measured by agriculture production indicator supported by higher cereal yield. Furthermore, such sectoral shift can be accelerated by well-functioning financial markets that facilitate the reallocation of economic resources and activities from low-productivity to high-productivity sectors (Calderon and Liu, 2003; Wampah, 2013).

From a more dynamic perspective, structural transformation can further be understood in relation to the need for an economy to be flexible enough to adapt its national context to the recent accelerating pace of change in the global environment effectively (Killick, 1995; Hassink, 2010). This perspective is firmly in line with development thinking of the New Structural Economics school of thought, which emphasises the importance of upgrading factor endowments, and such endowments can be altered in the long term through upgrading and technological innovation (Lin, 2012). In this development idea, greater potential in using internet penetration data for Sub-Saharan Africa was studied by Asongu, le Roux and Biekpe (2018). African countries may not necessarily develop new technology themselves but rather have the flexible process of adapting it from existing technology transfer mechanisms available to them (Stiglitz and Greenwald, 2014). In this respect, data from internet users as a proxy indicator is applied in this study. It should, however, be noted that without effective intergenerational transmission of human capital, technological possibilities cannot be materialised (Jones and Romer, 2009). Therefore, infant mortality data is included in the data set as a proxy indicator that reflects society's dual capability in terms of intergenerationality as well as quality health services. This is indeed a critical factor to incorporate the inclusiveness of the structural transformation process (Jain, 1985; Fayissa, 2001).

In their "Mathematics of structural transformation sector," Timmer et al. (2012) defined structural transformation with multiple processes as (a) a declining GDP share of agriculture accompanied by increasing productivity in the sector, (b) a rapid increase in the pace of urbanisation, (c) rising relative GDP shares of the manufacturing and service sectors and (d) a demographic transition from high to low rates of births and deaths. In line with Timmer's definition, the UN-led "Istanbul Programme of Action (IPoA) for the LDCs 2011–2020" specifically identified "improvement of health services by decreasing the infant mortality rate" as one of the essential driving factors of structural transformation (LDC IV Monitor, 2015, p.61). In sum, the study constructs a structural transformation index comprising the above seven variables to move towards a balanced multidimensional structural transformation.

The methodological approach employed by Armah and Baek (2015) is instructive in constructing the multi-dimensional index of structural transformation. They have used factor analysis to group those seven components of the structural transformation indicator into a single composite index where each factor is estimated using the maximum likelihood method to identify a set of strongly associated variables (Dempster, Laird and Rubin, 1977). A weighted composite index enables cross-country comparisons of the status of the structural transformation process and collapses several proxies of such transformation from one dependent variable into one variable while retaining most of the underlying information (Saltelli, 2007; Kelbore, 2014). The use of factor analysis to construct a weighted multi-dimensional structural transformation indicator thus involves the following steps.

The first step is to understand the underlying relationships by estimating the correlation between the variables. The correlation analysis indicates that the most highly correlated ones are between services value-added and the infant mortality rate in a negative manner, followed by between service value-added and manufacturing value-added in a positive fashion. Their estimation further employed a set of generally accepted criteria to identify factors in which the seven structural transformation indicators with high correlations form one underlying variable. (Kelbore, 2014). These sets are factors with eigenvalues closer to or greater than one, factors with individual contributions to the overall variance that exceed 10 per cent and factors with cumulative contributions to the overall variance that are greater than 70 per cent. Based on these, three factors were retained with the following characteristics: statistically significant at the 0.001 per cent level; goodness-of-fit, chi-square (31.471), Kaiser–Meyer–Olkin measure of sampling adequacy (0.680), and Bartlett's test of sphericity (953.938). In short, the three factors were identified whereas Factors 4, 5, 6 and 7 are not used for constructing the composite indicator due to a failure of meeting the criteria outlined earlier (see Table 5.1).

In the next step, the three factors using the Oblimin with the Kaiser normalisation method were rotated in order to estimate the relative

Table 5.1 Eigenvalues of the structural transformation data set

	Eigenvalues	% of variance explained	Cumulative %
Factor 1	2.887	41.240	41.240
Factor 2	1.214	17.349	58.589
Factor 3	0.959	13.695	72.284
Factor 4	0.753	10.764	83.048
Factor 5	0.531	7.579	90.627
Factor 6	0.371	5.305	95.932
Factor 7	0.285	4.068	100.000

Source: Armah and Baek (2015).
Notes: Extraction method is maximum likelihood. The eigenvalue is a measure of how much of the variance of the observed variables a factor explains. The eigenvalue of 2.8 for Factor 1 means that the factor explains as much variance as 2.8 of the observed variables

Table 5.2 Factor and weight analysis

	Factor loading			Squared factor loading (scaled to sum to unity)			Weight
	Factor 1	Factor 2	Factor 3	Factor 1	Factor 2	Factor 3	
SERVA	0.996	−0.127	0.170	0.703	0.012	0.038	0.292
MANVA	0.517	0.356	−0.160	0.189	0.092	0.034	0.118
CREDIT	0.205	0.763	−0.118	0.030	0.425	0.018	0.180
CREY	−0.048	0.618	0.028	0.002	0.278	0.001	0.109
MORTI	−0.323	−0.243	−0.499	0.074	0.043	0.326	0.116
INTU	−0.055	0.445	0.493	0.002	0.144	0.318	0.125
APIN	0.028	−0.088	0.450	0.001	0.006	0.265	0.059

Source: Armah and Baek (2015).
Notes: Extraction method is maximum likelihood. Rotation method is Oblimin with Kaiser normalisation. Rotation converged in seven iterations. CREY stands for cereal yield; APIN stands for agriculture gross per capita production index; SERVA stands for services value-added; INTU stands for internet users; MANVA stands for manufacturing value-added; CREDIT stands for domestic credit provided by financial sector; and MORTI stands for infant mortality rate.

contribution of each variable to each of the retained factors. Table 5.2 shows the rotated factor loadings and the three retained factors. Factor 1 contains two variables: services value-added (0.996) and manufacturing value-added (0.517) while the others have relatively smaller factor loadings (i.e. less than 0.500). Factor 2 includes only two variables with factor loadings exceeding 0.500: domestic credit (0.763) and cereal yield (0.618). Factor 3 is comprised of relatively lower factor loadings mainly due to their eigenvalue that does not exceed one. Notwithstanding, none of the factor loadings is greater than 0.500, the three variables were retained largely owing to being closer to 0.500:

infant mortality rate (−0.499), internet users (0.493) and agriculture production index (0.450).

In estimating the relative weight of each variable to a factor, Armah and Baek squared the factor loadings and scaled them to unity for the comparison purpose between variables. The results reveal three intermediate indicators. The first intermediate one includes service value-added (a weight of 0.703) and manufacturing value-added (a weight of 0.189) while the second set contains domestic credit (a weight of 0.425) and cereal yield (a weight of 0.278). Lastly, the third group has mortality rate (a weight of 0.326), internet use (a weight of 0.318) and agricultural production (a weight of 0.265). The relative contribution of each of the seven indicators to the structural transformation index, presented in the last column of Table 5.2, is computed as follows:

$$W_j = \sum STI_{ij}^2 \left/ \left(\begin{array}{c} \sum STI_{i1}^2 + \sum STI_{i2}^2 + \sum STI_{i3}^2 + \sum STI_{i4}^2 \\ + \sum STI_{i5}^2 + \sum STI_{i6}^2 + \sum STI_{i7}^2 \end{array} \right) \right.$$

where: W is estimated weight; STI represents the variables that comprise the structural transformation index; i is the factor dimension ($i = 1, 2, 3$); and j is variable dimension ($j = 1$ represents services value-added, 2 is manufacturing value-added, 3 is domestic credit provided by financial sector, 4 is cereal yield, 5 is infant mortality rate, 6 is internet users and 7 is agriculture gross per capita production index)

Services value-added contributes the largest weight to the structural transformation index (29.2 per cent), followed by domestic credit (18.0 per cent), internet use per 100 inhabitants (12.5 per cent), manufacturing value-added (11.8 per cent), infant mortality rate (11.6 per cent), cereal yield (10.9 per cent) and agriculture gross per capita production index (5.9 per cent). The composite structural transformation index (CSTI) is then computed as follows:

$$CSTI_{it} = \sum W_{cit} \cdot STI_{cit}$$

where c is indicator dimension ($c = 1 \ldots C$), i is country dimension ($i = 1 \ldots N$), t is time dimension ($t = 1 \ldots T$); W_{cit} is estimated weight; STI_{cit} represents the variables that comprise the structural transformation index; and $CSTI_{it}$ is composite structural transformation index.

116   *Integrated approach to sustainability*

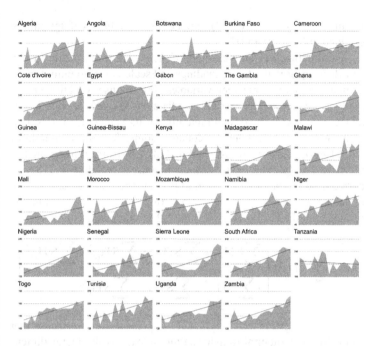

Figure 5.1 Evolution of the African structural transformation index.
Source: Armah and Baek (2015). Note: Grey line is the best-
fitting regression line.

In employing their modelling approach in measuring structural
transformation, Figure 5.1 displays how structural transformation in
29 African countries has evolved for the period 1995–2011. Overall,
structural transformation in the selected countries has improved by
41.4 per cent on average. It should, however, be acknowledged that
despite its advantage of capturing multi-dimensional features of
structural transformation for comparison analysis between countries,
composite indicator analysis could be exposed to limitations concerning sensitivity and the volatility of sub-indicators, which could mis-
lead non-robust policy implications (Freudenberg, 2003). The main
reason for the high volatility observed in the charts is that we have
applied our generalised weights (from 29 countries) to each of the
country's structural transformation formulas. Therefore, this analysis
would have less explanatory power of structural transformation performance by individual country but can be interpreted better for the
performance comparison among countries.

5.2 Theoretical contributions

This study makes contributions to the existing literature in several ways. A first original contribution has been to fill research gaps with respect to the nature and extent of the trade-offs and synergies among the three dimensions of sustainable development through the process of structural transformation. Investigating how the structural transformation process is affected by a comprehensive trinity of country change processes in relation to inclusive sustainable development discourse has so far received almost no significant attention. Indeed, capturing all these features in a single study has not been conducted in the literature. In this vein, one critical contribution to the literature lies in the empirical evidence that a silo approach that focuses on one dimension at the expense of another has a less optimal relationship to structural transformation, which challenges the dominant development paradigm of the *grow first, redistribute and clean up later* strategy.

Such a contribution feeds theoretically into the comprehensive framework for thinking about the ISD framework depicted in Figure 3.1. My investigation to explain the complexity of country change processes of inclusive sustainable development itself as one of the three important potential tensions was identified. This component also supported the idea that inequality-reducing policy dynamics (country change processes in Box 2), which can be influenced by the institutional feature of *path-dependence* (initial conditions in Box 3). Furthermore, the empirical results have confirmed that economic growth interventions (national development strategies in Box 1) interact with (re)distribution of income (country change processes in Box 2).

The greater contributions in explaining such systematic flows were made that country change processes (in Box 2), measured through three sets of sustainable development indicators, appear to be influenced by the normative idea of sustainable development, as represented by the Sustainable Development Goals (SDGs) (in Box 3). Together with the SDGs, doubling efforts to accelerate the process of structural transformation was identified as new development thinking mainly due to the countervailing trends facing most developing countries. These two competing development goals were translated into the normative frameworks (in Box 1) that could be adopted by national governments to inform country-specific development strategies.

In more detail, particularly for the case of African countries, the empirical results supported the inter-dynamics between country change processes and specific development strategies (interacting between Box 2 and Box 1) in a way that an integrated approach that takes into account the three dimensions would have the most beneficial relationship to these countries' structural transformation process. In other words, these findings emerged as being strongly valid when the structural effects (i.e. trade-offs and synergies between the three dimensions of sustainable development) were empirically identified in Chapter 4. In essence, the combination of global force to mainstream the sustainable development idea and a country's available resources and institutional capability (initial conditions in Box 3) would appear to determine such observed structural effects. Meanwhile, the technological possibilities available to African countries not only offer strategic options for national governments (Box 1), but they also influence country change processes (Box 2). In this context, these systematic flows will most likely determine whether it is feasible to achieve economic, social and environmental sustainability in the course of structural transformation of low-income countries.

5.3 Implications of the findings for practice

What are then some of the important policy implications from this study? As discussed, African countries have made substantial progress in advancing socioeconomic development in the past decade, but this progress has been uneven, and the benefits of rapid growth have not been broadly shared. Partly as a consequence, many African countries now have their own long-term (50 years) development framework aimed at structurally transforming economies and moving away from an exclusive focus on economic growth, which is in line with Agenda 2063.[2] Meanwhile, at the global level, the normative idea of sustainable development should encourage African governments to advance the economic, social and environmental dimensions of such development, which is consistent with the 2030 Agenda. It should be noted that central to Agenda 2063 is the structural transformation of the African continent, currently dependent on primary commodities and basic production policies, moving towards having more diversified economies with inclusive economic and political transformation, while the 2030 Agenda is a development plan of action for people, the planet and prosperity that is anchored by the principle of sustainable development in its three dimensions: social, economic and environmental (see Table 5.3).

Following the global adoption of both agendas, African governments began the process of designing national development planning frameworks that are aligned with both development initiatives. The new development agendas are timely, but their implementation will be no easy task for African countries. To be more specific, Agenda 2063 has many goals targets and indicators (i.e. seven aspirations, 20 goals, 34 priority areas, 171 national targets, 85 continental targets and 246 indicators). Meanwhile, the 2030

Table 5.3 The extent of convergence between the 2030 Agenda and Agenda 2063

2030 Agenda (SDGs)* by United Nations	Agenda 2063 by African Union
SDG 1: End poverty in all its forms everywhere	Goal 1: A high standard of living, quality of life and well-being for all
SDG 2: End hunger; achieve food security and improved nutrition, and promote sustainable agriculture	Goal 5: Modern agriculture for increased productivity and production
SDG 3: Ensure healthy lives and promote well-being for all at all ages	Goal 3: Healthy and well-nourished citizens
SDG 4: Ensure inclusive and equitable quality education and promote lifelong learning opportunities for all	Goal 2: Well-educated citizens and skills revolution underpinned by science, technology and innovation Goal 18: Engaged and empowered youth and children
SDG 5: Achieve gender equality and empower all women and girls	Goal 17: Full gender equality in all spheres of life
SDG 6: Ensure availability and sustainable management of water and sanitation for all	Goal 7: Environmentally sustainable climate resilient economies and communities
SDG 7: Ensure access to affordable, reliable, sustainable and modern energy for all	
SDG 8: Promote sustained, inclusive and sustainable economic growth, full and productive employment and decent work for all	Goal 4: Transformed economies and job creation
SDG 9: Build resilient infrastructure, promote inclusive and sustainable industrialisation and foster innovation	Goal 10: World-class infrastructure that criss-crosses Africa
SDG 11: Make cities and human settlements inclusive, safe, resilient and sustainable	
SDG 10: Reduce inequality within and among countries	Goal 1: A high standard of living, quality of life and well-being for all

(*Continued*)

Table 5.3 Continued

2030 Agenda (SDGs)* by United Nations	Agenda 2063 by African Union
SDG 12: Ensure sustainable consumption and production patterns	n/a
SDG 13: Take urgent action to combat climate change and its impacts	Goal 5: Environmentally sustainable climate resilient economies and communities
SDG 14: Conserve and sustainably use the oceans, seas and marine resources for sustainable development	Goal 6: Blue/ocean economy for accelerated economic growth
SDG 15: Protect, restore and promote sustainable use of terrestrial ecosystems, sustainably manage forests, combat desertification, halt and reverse land degradation and halt biodiversity loss	Goal 11: Democratic values, practices, universal principles of human rights, justice and the rule of law entrenched
SDG 16: Promote peaceful and inclusive societies for sustainable development, provide access to justice for all and build effective, accountable and inclusive institutions at all levels	Goal 12: Capable institutions and transformed leadership in place at all levels
	Goal 13: Peace, security and stability are preserved
	Goal 14: A stable and peaceful Africa
	Goal 15: A fully functional and operational African peace and security architecture
SDG 17: Strengthen the means of implementation and revitalise the global partnership for sustainable development	Goal 9: Key continental financial and monetary institutions established and functional
	Goal 19: Africa as a major partner in global affairs and peaceful co-existence
n/a	Goal 8: United Africa (federal or confederate)
n/a	Goal 16: African Cultural Renaissance is pre-eminent

Source: Baek (2019).

Note: Seventeen SDGs constitute the core of the 2030 Agenda for Sustainable Development.

Agenda also contains 17 goals, 169 targets and 230 indicators, many of which overlap with those of Agenda 2063, as already discussed in Box 2.1. Indeed, significant overlapping areas between these two exist. ECA (2017) has conducted a mapping analysis of the two agendas and concluded that in terms of target levels, four goals (SDGs 2, 5, 7 and 16) of the 2030 Agenda fully overlap with those of Agenda 2063. Detailed mapping results are presented in Figure 5.2. In sum, the goal-level mapping analysis sheds light on the exploration of potential correlations between structural transformation and sustainable development.

In this context, understanding and analysing the root causes of these policy challenges are of key importance to policymakers, which I believe the ISD framework could be/is able to support effectively. Of the many policy implications, I have chosen to focus on those related to the field of development planning, which can further be guided by the ISD framework, the criteria of which could then be referred to by policymakers.

In effect, mainstreaming the three dimensions of sustainable development into national planning frameworks is imperative for the successful implementation of the 2030 Agenda. Africa's development planning capacity, however, appears substantially weak; several of its countries are struggling to mainstream development priorities and policies in their national planning frameworks (ECA, 2017). This implies a need to break up institutional silos, thus strengthening sectoral (i.e. horizontal) and sub-national (i.e. vertical) coordination within and among implementing entities. Nonetheless, no analytical view on development planning would be intelligible without improved access to data, the reliability of which depends on the capacity of the relevant national statistics office.[3]

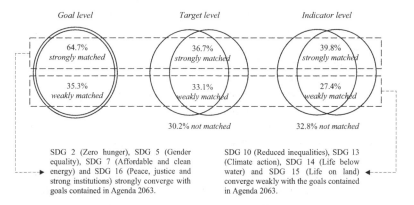

Figure 5.2 Convergence analysis between the 2030 Agenda and Agenda 2063.
Source: Baek (2019).

Notwithstanding valid concerns by policymakers about the trade-offs associated with environmentally driven development agendas, my empirical findings show that the total contribution of environmental initiatives to Africa's structural transformation agenda is greater than that of a structural transformation agenda led by economic growth strategies. The results have also explained that prioritising social development in most African countries may be the most expeditious pathway to achieving structural transformation. It is important to note that my empirical evidence does not suggest that a successful structural transformation programme requires an exclusive focus on the social dimension. What it does imply is that a structural transformation initiative led by social development is more catalytic in terms of its impact. This book thus provides policymakers with a useful framework for prioritising and sequencing policy interventions to achieve the normative agenda for sustainable development and to advance their structural transformation objectives (see Box 5.2).

BOX 5.2   ILLUSTRATIVE POLICY SIMULATIONS OF ALTERNATIVE STRUCTURAL TRANSFORMATION STRATEGIES

A simple mathematical simulation is conducted to support my research findings as an integrated approach towards sustainable structural transformation. To demonstrate the concept of "transformation strategies with endogenous long-term growth performance possibilities," my simulations simply assume that there are three types of structural transformation: *Dirty transformation* (D); *Green transformation* (G); and *Zero transformation* (Z). The first type is defined as being unsustainable development, where the economy is transformed without consideration of environmental quality. The second type is realised through the synergy effect between economic value and environmental conservation. Meanwhile, the third strategy targets an improvement to environmental quality, which crucially offsets the economic transformation process (trade-offs effect). Finally, the dotted line represents a unit of time, which is one year and hence, this is an annualised concept, such that every year a country should design its targeted intervention for what types of transformation it wants to pursue (see Figure 5.3).

For the vertical axis, α_t is defined as structural transformation outcome in year t, while $\Delta\alpha_t$ are the changes in structural transformation outcomes between α_t and α_{t-1}. Hence, α_t can be specified as follows:

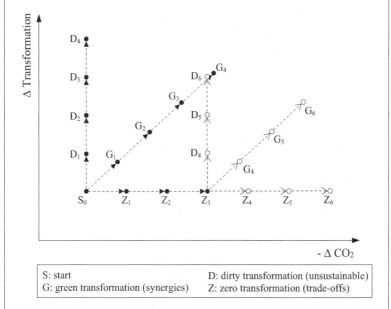

| S: start | D: dirty transformation (unsustainable) |
| G: green transformation (synergies) | Z: zero transformation (trade-offs) |

Figure 5.3 Transformation strategies with endogenous long-term growth performance possibilities.

$$\alpha_t = \alpha_{t-1} + \left(\alpha_{t-1} \times \Delta\alpha_t\right)$$

As for the environment aspect (horizontal axis), carbon dioxide emissions as per cent of α_t can be defined to be $\prod\beta_t$, which is the baseline carbon dioxide emissions required to support the size of a transformative economy. Furthermore, additional carbon dioxide emissions (or reduction of the emissions) that depend on the type of policy intervention are included as $(\cap\beta_t)$. The sum of both the baseline and policy-driven carbon dioxide emissions can be the accumulated carbon dioxide emissions in year t.

Therefore, $\Delta\beta_t$ can be expressed as:

$$\Delta\beta_t = \left(\alpha_t \times \prod\beta_t\right) \times \left(1 + \Delta\cap\beta_t\right)$$

This formula can be rearranged for cumulative carbon dioxide emissions in year t as:

$$\beta_t = \left(\alpha_t \times \prod\beta_t\right) \times \left(1 + \Delta\cap\beta_t\right) + \beta_{t-1}$$

Now, five policy simulations are run for 30 years: the above three transformation types: (1) dirty, (2) green and (3) zero transformations along with (4) dirty transformation for 15 years, then zero transformation for the rest as well as (5) zero transformation for 15 years and then dirty transformation for the rest. Even though appearing to be extreme cases, two mixed policy interventions are simulated for the purpose of comparison.

The simulation results show that the dirty transformation policies over 30 years generate the greatest transformative outcomes while posing the biggest environmental risk (see Figure 5.4). In contrast, the zero transformative policy is associated with minimal impacts on transformation, while also promoting the greatest environmental conservation. In the middle stage, green transformation is placed as being in between transformative outcomes and environmental degradation. This can be considered as minimising trade-off effects.

When zero interventions are implemented for the first half of the simulated period, followed by dirty transformative ones for the remaining years, while the structural transformation level is simulated to being a similar level to that generated by the dirty-zero transformation policy, its carbon dioxide emissions level is far below and even below that of the green transformation interventions. This result implies that the *law of accelerating returns* (Kurzweil, 2005) could

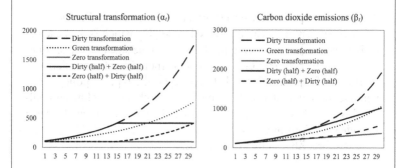

Figure 5.4 Simulations results on five structural transformation strategies.
Notes: $\Delta\alpha_t$ for dirty, green and zero transformation is assumed to be 10 per cent, the root square of 100 per cent and zero per cent, respectively; $\prod\beta_t$ is assumed to be 10 per cent for all the policy scenarios; and finally, $\Delta\beta_t$ for dirty, green and zero transformation is assumed to be zero per cent, the root square of 100 per cent and 10 per cent, respectively.

play a role in this simulation case or in other words, it can be interpreted as a *path-dependence* feature in the sense that a country tends to choose its previously implemented policies.

In this regard, the sooner an environmental programme is implemented, the greater the synergy effects that will be captured. In other words, policymakers may need to take into account that *clean first and grow later* can be a better strategic stance than *grow first and clean up later*, and more critically, that development planning for prioritising and sequencing policy interventions at this point in time will determine what types of transformation will be achieved in the future.

From more of a policy standpoint, regarding African countries, a study conducted by Armah and Baek (2018) has pointed to rising primary school enrolment; however, the skills profile of students is skewed towards the arts and humanities with disproportionately low representation in the fields of science and technology. The quality of educational facilities, as well as the alignment of skills to the requisite needs of the labour market, are other areas of concern. Health indicators have also improved markedly, with substantial declines in child and maternal mortality due in part to increased access to skilled birth attendants, vaccinations and a decline in adolescent birth rates. Nevertheless, overall, access to quality healthcare services is limited. A skilled and healthy workforce will most likely emigrate for better career opportunities if the conditions for employment and livelihood generation are limited. Despite its energy endowments, access to energy in Africa is abysmally low and poses a key constraint to industrialisation, enterprise development and employment creation. Leveraging the continent's energy potential will be critical for promoting value addition, industrial growth and employment.

The potential for such growth to be inclusive will be further enhanced through measures to promote financial inclusion by facilitating access to financial services by the currently unbanked and underserved segments of the population. The rapid increase in access to mobile phones, coupled with innovations in information, communication and technology (ICT) that make it possible for individuals to have wireless access to financial services, have made Africa a leader in mobile account holders. Policymakers can advance inclusive growth by further leveraging the opportunities provided by innovations in mobile telephony.

Nonetheless, the importance of manufacturing sector development should not be underestimated, as it still offers the possibility of both job and income creation, particularly when countries are at a relatively low-income level (UNIDO, 2017). In fact, the potential of manufacturing sectors with the use of green technologies (e.g. renewable energy equipment) will be greater, particularly for countries richer in natural resources (IRENA and ESCWA, 2018).

Mainstreamed into the manufacturing sector, and even into the services one too, multi-dimensional implications derived from recent technological change, particularly digital technologies, should be taken into account when it comes to national industrial policy frameworks that entail structural transformation (Dengler and Matthes, 2018). In other words, such transformation will affect the conventional development equation and further influence shaping somewhat different pathways towards structural transformation. It should be noted that digital-technology-led transformation could raise the overall level of productivity and contribute to creating decent jobs while easing access to quality public services (Lundvall et al., 2011). In particular, it could expand opportunities for technological leapfrogging of less technologically developed countries. In order to maximise those potential benefits, the three grounding factors need to be in place or at least efforts made (e.g. development plans) for them to be implemented.

The first, and arguably most important of these grounding factors, is access to quality digital infrastructure. Wider access to affordable digital infrastructure will be essential in enabling inclusiveness throughout society, which would strengthen national capacity to leapfrog in terms of the acceptance and integration of new technology in society (Johnson and Andersen, 2012). It is particularly relevant in boosting opportunities for women and girls to enhance their knowledge, economic power and independence, among others, thus collectively creating additional economic resources to accelerate the process of structural transformation in developing countries (UN, 2021a).

The second grounding factor concerns digital skills. Improving digital literacy is closely associated with the nexus between human capital and digital transformation (UN, 2021b). Broadly speaking, introducing lifelong and high-quality digital learning courses can enhance the employability of economically active populations in professions and activities during the digital transformation era. Strengthened digital capacity requires adopting (or upgrading, if already in existence) the science, technology, engineering and mathematics (STEM) curricula in higher education, which needs to be implemented in parallel with designing a national strategy in facilitating investment in technology-intensive sectors, especially small and medium-sized enterprises (SMEs) and local businesses (UN, 2018).

Finally, timely and effective regulations with incentives should be set and implemented. Digital technologies could facilitate a sectoral transition (in individual sectors or across sectors) (Baek, 2018). For instance, an agri-culture-led transformation can be promoted by the deployment of renewable energy systems, and irrigation practices with the use of big data on weather patterns, among others. Another example can be related to economies of scale in industry when policies supporting the application of digital technologies (e.g. the Internet of Things) are emphasised. Doing so would strengthen back-wards and forwards linkages and the development of more sophisticated pro-duction lines while raising productivity in the services sector as well.

5.4 Limitations and future research

There are a number of limitations I have encountered during the research that are also very closely related to my suggestion for future research, which can in turn extend or improve this study.

First, despite substantive contributions to existing literature through contextualising the systematic flows reflected in the ISD framework, the two country change processes (i.e. the growth–environment nexus and the inequality–environment nexus) have not been empirically explored yet, to which a similar methodology for the inequality–growth nexus can be applied. These empirically untold stories may limit a comprehen-sive attempt to explain the whole story embedded in the ISD framework. Furthermore, the scope of the study initially set may also restrain the ISD framework's explanatory power on the complex dynamics in play: it was initially assumed that the role of technological progress was an exogenous variable mainly because endogenising it into the ISD framework would ren-der empirical work far more complex.

Second, the financial aspect is not incorporated in the ISD framework, namely financing for development (FfD). However, this is indeed one of the important elements that has been integrated into the development policy dis-course at both global and national levels. Notably, the Addis Ababa Action Agenda (AAAA)[4] offers a new global framework for FfD that aligns all financing flows and policies with economic, social and environmental priori-ties. This is aimed at ensuring that financing is stable and sustainable, while the AAAA particularly urges that the financial resources required for achieving the SDGs considerably exceed what is currently available. UNCTAD (2018) has also pointed out that the total investment needs for developing countries to realise the 2030 Agenda are estimated at about US\$3.9 trillion per year, with current investment levels falling short of that by some US\$1.4 trillion. Given the additional need for financial resources to realise Agenda 2063, achiev-ing these two normative agendas with a *business-as-usual* approach remains highly unlikely. In this context, further studies will be needed to provide more concrete guidelines to integrating the financial resources aspect into the ISD framework so as to build the comprehensive theoretical framework that takes into account both the policymaking capacity and financial aspects together.

On the technical side, there are a couple of issues that I strongly believe are areas for improvement that must be addressed. For instance, the limited number of observations for my modelling exercises may have influenced the empirical results. Hence, more advanced robustness tests would need to be conducted, e.g. confirmatory factor analysis. Additionally, many parts of the developing country group are restrained by the limited number of observations (due to data unavailability), which would have inevitably biased the sample and the results. In this regard, my attempt to advance some interesting generalisations that highlight empirical regularities can be effective value-added interventions to ongoing scholarly communications in this field, if such data challenges were substantially resolved. Again, access to data on a broader range of indicators would further enhance the quality and robustness of the latent constructs.

To reiterate a number of limitations (discussed in Chapter 2), the ISD framework could be extended to address the challenges of: balancing macroeconomic stability with structural transformation (Nissanke, 2019); mainstreaming the three dimensions of sustainable development into national planning frameworks (Fischer et al., 2015); and mutually reinforcing the role of institutions in supporting sustainable transformation (Osman, Alexiou and Tsaliki, 2012). Furthermore, the role of regional intervention in the national development framework deserves future study because it would not only play the role of linking up national policies to the normative goals, but it would also speed up the process of interactions between national and global dimensions. For instance, AUC (African Union Commission), AfDB (African Development Bank) and ECA (Economic Commission for Africa) as far as the African context is concerned can offer capacity-building assistance of policymaking and development planning to countries, especially poor and small ones. Filling all these gaps to advance the ISD framework would, however, require a completely different set of literature compared with that covered in this study.[5]

5.5 Concluding thoughts

This book has involved drawing on a large area of scholarly work and broad ideas about development in a state of constant flux, with influential thinkers driving the never-ending evaluation of the development discourse, incorporating theories of modernisation, endogenous growth, globalisation and neoliberalism, among others. Yet its basic premises are straightforward, being mainly concerned with how economic growth, equality/inclusion and environmental sustainability goals are, should be and can be jointly managed through the process of structural transformation, with particular reference to low-income countries.

In so doing, I have explored an untold story in which many developing countries today, especially in Africa, are pursuing one or both of the following policy agendas in their policy mix as they strive towards sustainable transformation: (1) a global normative agenda moving away from traditional patterns of economic growth and towards a greater emphasis on sustainable development; and (2) a context-dependent national development policy agenda that entails the achievement of a more radical structural transformation that goes beyond economic growth based on the current international division of labour. Having identified these two overlapping policy agendas, this study was theoretically and empirically concerned about how efforts to advance the three dimensions of sustainable development, namely economic growth, inequality and environmental aspects, affect the process of structural transformation.

My empirical findings suggested that a silo approach that focuses on one dimension at the expense of another does not deliver effective structural transformation, which challenges the dominant development paradigm of the *grow first, redistribute and clean up later* strategy. Rather, an inclusive and sustainable structural transformation agenda would require tackling the economic, social and environmental dimensions of sustainable development in an integrated way. In particular, a structural equation modelling approach has pointed out that the total contribution of environmental initiatives to Africa's structural transformation agenda is greater than that of a structural transformation agenda led by economic growth strategies. This econometric approach also explained that prioritising social development in African countries may be the most expeditious pathway to structural transformation.

In short, under the normative idea of inclusive sustainable development largely impacting on low-income countries, accelerating the process of structural transformation would substantially hinge upon policy interventions, especially a development planning framework for an integrated and coherent approach to sustainable development. Mindful of this, a type of structural transformation that developing countries will most likely want will be determined not exogenously, but endogenously. In the next few decades, sustainable structural transformation of low-income countries will, thus, be greatly shaped by development planning strategies of integrating, prioritising and/or sequencing policy interventions among the three dimensions of sustainable development.

Notes

1 In several respects, the New Structural Economics paradigm speaks to the development realities of most African economies (Lin, 2012), which tend to score

relatively low on investment, savings and technological innovation indicators. Sub-Saharan African countries on average have lower savings and investment to GDP ratios than other regions of the world and the technological content of their manufactured exports is also relatively lower than the global average, due in part to limited investments in research and development (Armah and Baek, 2018).

2 "In January 2015, the Heads of State and Government of the African Union adopted Agenda 2063, a strategic framework for inclusive growth and sustainable development in Africa, and a strategy to optimise the use of the continent's resources for the benefit of all Africans" (ECA et al., 2016, pp.29).

3 There have been a number of Africa's statistical capacity improvement initiatives supported by development partners, e.g. Strategy for the Harmonization of Statistics in Africa (SHaSA) – launched in 2010 under the joint aegis of ECA, AfDB and AUC, Economic and Statistical Observatory for Sub-Saharan Africa (AFRISTAT) and Pan-African Institute for Statistics (STATAFRIC), among others.

4 This is the outcome document from the Financial for Development conference held in Addis Ababa from 13 to 16 July 2015.

5 For example, Wannop and Cherry (1994), Simmons (1999), Counsell and Haughton (2003), Haughton and Counsell (2004), Elder, Bengtsson and Akenji (2016), Kapfudzaruwa et al. (2017) and Perry and García (2017).

References

Armah, B. and Baek, S.J., 2015. Can the SDGs promote structural transformation in Africa? An empirical analysis. *Development*, 58(4), pp.473–491.

Armah, B. and Baek, S.J., 2018. Three interventions to foster sustainable transformation in Africa. *Journal of Social, Political and Economic Studies*, 43(1–2), pp.3–25.

Asongu, S.A., le Roux, S. and Biekpe, N., 2018. Enhancing ICT for environmental sustainability in sub-Saharan Africa. *Technological Forecasting and Social Change*, 127, pp.209–216.

Baek, S.J., 2018. *The political economy of neo-modernisation: Rethinking the dynamics of technology, development and inequality*. London: Palgrave Macmillan.

Baek, S.J., 2019. Cooperating in Africa's sustainable structural transformation: Policymaking capacity and the role of emerging economies. *International Development Planning Review*, 41(4), pp.419–434.

Calderon, C. and Liu, L., 2003. The direction of causality between financial development and economic growth. *Journal of Development Economics*, 72(1), pp.321–334.

Christiaensen, L., Demery, L. and Kuhl, J., 2011. The (evolving) role of agriculture in poverty reduction: An empirical perspective. *Journal of Development Economics*, 98(2), pp.239–254.

Counsell, D and Haughton, G., 2003. Regional planning in transition: Planning for growth and sustainable development in two contrasting regions. *Environment and Planning*, C21, pp.225–239.

Dabla-Norris, E., Thomas, A., Garcia-Verdu, R. and Chen, Y., 2013. *Benchmarking structural transformation across the world*, IMF Working Paper (WP/13/176). Available from: https://www.imf.org/~/media/Websites/IMF/imported-fulltext -pdf/external/pubs/ft/wp/2013/_wp13176.ashx [Accessed 10 November 2015].

Dempster, A.P., Laird, N.M. and Rubin, D.B., 1977. Maximum likelihood from incomplete data via the EM algorithm. *Journal of the Royal Statistical Society Series B (Methodological)*, 39(1), pp.1–38.

Dengler, K. and Matthes, B., 2018. The impacts of digital transformation on the labor market: Substitution potentials of occupations in Germany. *Technological Forecasting and Social Change*, 137, pp.304–316.

ECA (Economic Commission for Africa), 2017. *Integrating agenda 2063 and 2030 agenda for sustainable development into national development plans: Emerging issues for African least developed countries.* Addis Ababa: ECA.

ECA, AUC (African Union Commission), AfDB (African Development Bank) and UNDP (United Nations Development Programme), 2016. *MDGs to agenda 2063/ SDGs transition report 2016: Towards an integrated and coherent approach to sustainable development in Africa.* Addis Ababa: ECA.

Elder, M., Bengtsson, M. and Akenji, L., 2016. An optimistic analysis of the means of implementation for sustainable development goals: Thinking about goals as means. *Sustainability*, 8(9), pp.962–986.

Fayissa, B., 2001. The determinants of infant and child mortality in developing countries: The case of Sub-Sahara Africa. *Review of Black Political Economy*, 29(2), pp.83–100.

Fischer, J., Gardner, T.A., Bennett, E.M., Balvanera, P., Biggs, R., Carpenter, S., Daw, T., Folke, C., Hill, R., Hughes, T.P., Luthe, T., Maass, M., Meacham, M., Norstrom, A.V., Peterson, G., Queiroz, C., Seppelt, R., Spierenburg, M. and Tenhunen, J., 2015. Advancing sustainability through mainstreaming a social-ecological systems perspective. *Current Opinion in Environmental Sustainability*, 14, pp.144–149.

Freudenberg, M., 2003. *Composite indicators of country performance: A critical assessment*, DSTI/DOC(2003)16. Paris: OECD. Available from: https://www .oecd-ilibrary.org/docserver/405566708255.pdf?expires=1583940263&id=id &accname=guest&checksum=FB3D0956849ED93B0E244CE0DD0AD12B [Accessed 29 February 2020].

Hassink, R., 2010. Regional resilience: A promising concept to explain differences in regional economic adaptability? *Cambridge Journal of Regions, Economy and Society*, 3(1), pp.45–58.

Haughton, G. and Counsell, D., 2004. Regions and sustainable development: Regional planning matters. *Geographical Journal*, 70(2), pp.135–145.

Herrendorf, B., Rogerson, R. and Valentinyi, Á., 2013. Two perspectives on preferences and structural transformation. *American Economic Review*, 103(7), pp.2752–2789.

IRENA (International Renewable Energy Agency) and ESCWA (Economic and Social Commission for Western Asia), 2018. *Evaluating renewable energy manufacturing potential in the Arab region*: Jordan, Lebanon, United Arab Emirates. Abu Dhabi: IRENA.

132   *Integrated approach to sustainability*

Jain, A.K., 1985. The impact of development and population policies on fertility in India. *Studies in Family Planning*, 16(4), pp.181–198.

Johnson, B. and Andersen, A.D., 2012. Learning, innovation and inclusive development: *New perspectives on economic development strategy and development aid*. Aalborg Universitetsforlag (Globelics Thematic Report Vol. 2011/2012).

Jones, C.I. and Romer, R.M. 2009. *The new Kaldor facts: Ideas, institutions, population, and human capital*, NBER Working Paper No. 15094. Cambridge, MA: National Bureau of Economic Research.

Kapfudzaruwa, F., Kanie, N., Weinberger, K., Mallee, H. and Ishii, A., 2017. *The sustainable development goals and regional institutions: Exploring their role in Asia and the Pacific*. Tokyo: UNU-IAS (Policy Brief-No.11).

Kelbore, Z.G., 2014. *Multidimensional structural transformation index: A new measure of development*, MPRA Paper No. 62920 [Online]. Available from: https://mpra.ub.uni-muenchen.de/62920/1/MPRA_paper_62920.pdf [Accessed 22 September 2015].

Killick, T., 1995. *The flexible economy: Causes and consequences of the adaptability of national economies*. London: Routledge.

LDC IV Monitor, 2015. *Istanbul programme of action for the LDCs (2011–2020): Monitoring deliverables, tracking progress: Analytical perspectives*. London: Commonwealth Secretariat.

Lin, J., 2012. *New structural economics: A framework for rethinking development and policy*. Washington, DC: World Bank.

Lundvall, B.A., Joseph, K.J., Chaminade, C. and Vang, J., 2011. *Handbook of innovation systems and developing countries: Building domestic capabilities in a global setting*. Cheltenham: Elgar.

Nissanke, M., 2019. Exploring macroeconomic frameworks conducive to structural transformation of sub-Saharan African economies. *Structural Change and Economic Dynamics*, 48, pp.103–116.

Osman, R.H., Alexiou, C. and Tsaliki, P., 2012. The role of institutions in economic development: Evidence from 27 Sub-Saharan African countries. *International Journal of Social Economics*, 39(1/2), pp.142–160.

Perry, G. and García, E., 2017. The influence of multilateral development institutions on Latin American development strategies. In: G. Carbonnier, H. Campodónico and S.T. Vázquez, eds. *Alternative pathways to sustainable development: Lessons from Latin America*. International Development Policy series No.9 (Geneva, Boston: Graduate Institute Publications, Brill-Nijhoff), pp.199–231.

Saltelli, A., 2007. Composite indicators between analysis and advocacy. *Social Indicators Research*, 81(1), pp.65–77.

Simmons, M., 1999. The revival of regional planning. *Town Planning Review*, 70(3), pp.159–172.

Stiglitz, J.E. and Greenwald, B.C., 2014. *Creating a learning society: A new approach to growth, development, and social progress*. New York: Columbia University Press.

Timmer, C.P., Badiane, M.M.O., Rodrik, D., Binswanger-Mkhize, H. and Wouterse, F., 2012. *Patterns of growth and structural transformation in Africa: Trends and lessons for future development strategies*, IFPRI Thematic Research Note 2. Washington, DC: International Food Policy Research Institute. Available from: http://www.ifpri.org/cdmref/p15738coll2/id/126946/filename/127157.pdf [Accessed 28 June 2015].

UN (United Nations), 2018. *World economic and social survey 2018: Frontier technologies for sustainable development*. New York: UN/DESA (ST/ESA/370).

UN, 2021a. *Leveraging digital technologies for social inclusion*. New York: UN/ DESA (Policy Brief #92). Available from: https://www.un.org/development/desa /dpad/publication/un-desa-policy-brief-92-leveraging-digital-technologies-for -social-inclusion [Accessed 17 September 2021].

UN, 2021b. *Unlocking human capital potential in Kuwait as global actor in the knowledge economy*. Kuwait: UN. Available from: https://kuwait.un.org/en/ download/76503/134060 [Accessed 10 September 2021].

UNCTAD (United Nations Conference on Trade and Development), 2018. *Scaling up finance for the sustainable development goals: Experimenting with models of multilateral development banking*. Geneva: UNCTAD.

UNIDO (United Nations Industrial Development Organization), 2017. *Structural change for inclusive and sustainable industrial development*. Vienna: UNIDO.

Wampah, H.A.K., 2013. What does it take to build a stable and efficient financial sector for sustaining growth and structural transformation in Africa? In: D. Willem te Velde and S. Griffith-Jones, eds. *Sustaining growth and structural transformation in Africa: How can a stable and efficient financial sector help?* London: Overseas Development Institute.

Wannop, U. and Cherry, G., 1994. The development of regional planning in the United Kingdom. *Planning Perspectives*, 9(1), pp.29–60.

Index

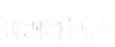

9781032195865